After an early childhood in Pretoria, Nick Lithgow reported for National Service duty with the SADF. This saw him deploying to the Border as an infantry soldier with a brief interlude to Pretoria for pilot assessment. Much to his surprise, Nick was called forward for pilot training and this saw him learning his craft on the Harvard and Impala. He soon graduated to rotary aircraft with the Alouette and shortly thereafter, in 1979, Nick became a Puma pilot. At the height of the South African Border War, Nick flew Puma helicopters across the 'Operational Area' conducting troop moves, casevacs, fighting patrols with special forces and more. In the Drakensburg mountain range Nick conducted daring cliff rescues, whilst at sea he was instrumental in a number of difficult rescues. Nick now lives in Durban, South Africa, with business interests in Johannesburg. He continues to love anything to do with aviation.

For my children Angie and Andrew, and my good buddy Martin van Straten.

FALLEN BRETHREN

To all our fallen brethren lost
Immortal words with honour trust
We bear your guiding lamp with pride
With tears and smiles, remembered thus
And when the lamp flames flicker, we know
Your spirits are always close to us – NL

Proceeds from this book will be donated to the South African Air Force Association NPO 083-072

LZ HOT!

Flying South Africa's Border War

Nick Lithgow

Helion & Company

G G Books UK

Co-published in 2012 by:

Helion & Company Limited
26 Willow Road
Solihull
West Midlands B91 1UE
England
Tel. 0121 705 3393
Fax 0121 711 4075
Email: info@helion.co.uk
Website: www.helion.co.uk

and

GG Books UK
Rugby
Warwickshire
Tel: 07921 709307
Website: www.30degreessouth.co.uk

Designed and typeset by Farr out Publications, Wokingham, Berkshire
Cover designed by Euan Carter, Leicester (www.euancarter.com)
Printed by Henry Ling Ltd, Dorchester, Dorset

Text © Nick Lithgow 2012
Photographs as individually credited
Cover photograph © Al J. Venter

ISBN 978-1-908916-59-4

British Library Cataloguing-in-Publication Data.
A catalogue record for this book is available from the British Library.

All rights reserved. No part of this publication may be reproduced, stored in a retrieval system,or transmitted, in any form, or by any means, electronic, mechanical, photocopying, recording or otherwise, without the express written consent of Helion & Company Limited and GG Books.

For details of other military history titles published by Helion & Company Limited contact the above address, or visit our website: http://www.helion.co.uk.

We always welcome receiving book proposals from prospective authors.

Contents

List of Illustrations

Foreword

What a great book! Instead of boring us with only the facts, the facts and more of the facts (or so called!), Nick has applied the human element that has been missing so long in the helicopter stories; at last! From his basics in the army to being a full blooded chopper pilot in the largest bush war in Southern Africa, he has painted a picture here that allows the reader to relax in the comfort of home, hotel, or wherever, and read the humorous (sometimes hilarious!) accounts of how the brave chopper boys there did their bit in keeping the home front safe from the vagaries of war!

As is the custom with helicopter pilots, modesty is somehow inbred, (not quietness, mind you!) so when reading the 'episodes' one should really try to imagine it in reality – this was no game. It was real war, serious in the way wars need to be. More chopper boys were lost in the war than any other types. Hence, as Nick mentions, more medals were handed out to the chopper boys than to any other mustering. In fact, the very first SADF Honoris Crux for bravery was earned by a helicopter pilot. But, as it is with such things, humour keeps one 'sane' or from going "bossies" (bush-mad) along the way, particularly when the going gets tough … and it does. There was and is a true camaraderie in the chopper fraternity and Nick brings this to the fore in his many examples of teamwork, hard at times, fun at others.

In certain ways I liken this work to *Eagle Day* by Richard Collier. Collier's book covers just six weeks during the Battle of Britain and is recorded in vivid detail, telling it how it was, not buffing it up with unseemly shine. Nick's work is over years, but the same pattern prevails – the way the chopper boys are, humorous, hard, naughty (but nice!), and yet so caring for their fellow men (mostly also chopper boys, of course!). The demeanour of the Battle of Britain crews was seemingly very carefree, probably because they flew in danger so often that seriousness of being earnest would have been a stumbling block. Things have changed in today's world, but that same indomitable spirit was what the chopper boys took over from World War II fighter pilots, for our bush war. They went in first, did the most, lost the most, and those that survived, came out last, with heads held high and with a myriad accolades.

Examples of this spirit are legion, but suffice to recall one incident that parallels the same thing in Collier's book, when the mess kitchen was locked on return of the chopper boys from an operation and no one could open up, they took that duty upon themselves, rather robustly, so that the boys could be fed. Broken locks aside, the Officers Commanding in those halcyon days of the bush war earned much credit for (mostly) standing by the chopper boys when they got up to antics which would normally have had stern disciplinary consequences!

Well done Nick! The picture is so real that it transported me back easily to those wonderful days of dust and the smell of aviation turbine fuel! You have brought it to life without having to go over-the-top, without having to "manufacture" anecdotes. This is a real story and I know that readers will enjoy it thoroughly. It is a story that one can go back to – get more of, enjoy again! I salute Nick for making the effort and getting it done, and done so well, so realistically! This will become a great piece of Africana, and may your talent be just like the helicopters we so love – forever rising, vertically! It is great being a chopper boy and yes Nick, I would also ask God for more of the same if I had the opportunity!

Brigadier General Peter 'Monster' Wilkins, SAAF (Rtd), AFC, SCM, MMM,
Chief Pilot and Head of Flight Operations
Starlite Aviation South Africa and Ireland

Acknowledgements

I must thank the SAAF for giving me the best damn job I ever had and opening the door to what must be the craziest fraternity of professional people on the planet, the chopper pilots. Many thanks to Louis Nel, Janine Noel-Barham and Brigadier John Boardman (retd.) who made this publication possible and to the Ballito Writers Guild for their support and encouragement.

Glossary and List of Abbreviations

A20	Portable field radio
Ack-ack	Anti-aircraft field gun (Russian cal. 23mm)
AK47	Kalashnikov AK47 assault rifle (Russian cal. 7.62mm)
Alouette	Aerospatiale Alouette III light helicopter
AVGAS	Aviation grade petroleum
AVTUR	Aviation grade turbine fuel
Bakkie	Utility vehicle
Bats	ParaBats or paratroopers
Browns	Combat fatigues
C130/Hercules	Lockheed C130 tactical transport aircraft
C160/Transall	Transport Allianz C160 tactical transport aircraft
Casevac	Casualty evacuation
Chopper	Helicopter
CO	Candidate Officer
Contact	Engaging the enemy
Collective	Helicopter throttle
Cyclic	Helicopter joystick
Dak/Dakota	Douglas DC3 transport aircraft ('goony bird', 'vomit comet')
DB	Detention Barracks
Dispersal area	*See* hardstand
Dominee	Church minister
ELT	Emergency Locator Transmitter
FM	Frequency modulated radio
Flossie	Either C130 or C160 transport aircraft
GF	General flying area
Gharry, Bakkie	Usually a Land Rover 110 or Toyota Hilux
Gunship	Alouette 3 fitted with a side mounted 20mm cannon
Hardstand	*See* dispersal area

Imp	Atlas Impala trainer and light ground attack jet
Knots	Nautical miles per hour i.e. 100 knots = 115 miles per hour = 184 kilometres per hour
MAOT	Mobile Air Operations Team
MP	Military policeman
Mielie	Corn cob
Mirage	Dassault Mirage 3 and F1 jet fighters
OC	Officer Commanding
Oom	Uncle
Ops	Operations co-ordinating personnel
Ordnance	Military combat hardware
ParaBats	ParaBats or paratroopers
Phos grenade	White phosphorous incendiary hand grenade
PT	Physical training
Puma	Aerospatiale SA 332 Puma medium lift helicopter
Ratel	Armoured personnel carrier (Eng: Honey badger)
Rat-packs	Ration packs
Recces	Reconnaissance Corps troops
Revetment	Large sand wall to protect military equipment and installations
R1	Fabrique Nationale assault rifle (Belgian cal: 7.62mm)
R4	Assault rifle (South African cal: 5.56mm)
RPG	Rocket propelled grenade (Russian)
SAAF	South African Air Force
SADF	South African Defence Force
SWAPO	South West African People's Organization
SAM	Surface to Air Missile
SAM 7	Russian shoulder-launched anti-aircraft heat seeking missile
Thunderflash	Practice hand grenade, like a large firecracker
U/S	Unservicable

32 Battalion	Owambo local population troops trained by S.A.D.F.
50 (five-oh) Browning	Mounted machine gun cal: 12.7mm

Chopper/military slang

Aapkak, apeshit	Go crazy, berserk
Afkak	Shitting off
Babalas	Hangover
Bliksem, bliksemse	Cursed
Boerewors	Traditional farmer's sausage
Bossies, bosbefok	Crazy, as in combat fatigue
Bosvark	Bush pig
Civvy	Civilian
Civvy street	Civilian life
Clag, clagged in	Cloud, clouded over
Clusterfuck	Blunder, making a mistake as a group
Cocksparrow	Junior pilot
Dagga	Cannabis
Die grens (the border)	SWA/Namibia operational area
Die kas	Detention Barracks/Military prison
Donnerse	Thundering or bloody
Doos (Eng: box)	Fool, idiot
Down on power	Feeling low, depressed, hung over
Draadkar	Wire car – affectionate name for the Alo 3
Dronk verdriet	Crying when drunk
Drop your pose	Come down to earth
Gasóleo	Diesel oil
Gook	Americanization of enemy
Gyppo	Duck and dive
Gyppo gat	Lazy arse
Kak sleg	Very poor, bad
Kakking off	Uncomfortable
Kas	Small metal cupboard
Kit form	Broken, damaged
Klap it	Go for it
Klapping it	Busy with a task, going flat out
Kokarot	Cockroach

Kop toe	Headstrong
Mielie	Maize
Miracle	Mirage jet fighter
Moerkas	Coffin, dead
Moer toe	Broken or damaged
Naai beat	Stand guard
Natdroom	Wet dream
Oom	Uncle
Oumanne	Experienced troops
Paraat	Smart, conscientious
Piss on (a person's) battery	Insult or reprimand someone
Pongo	Anyone in the army
Pootjie	Cast iron cooking pot with three legs
Rip the ring out	Go overboard, reckless
Samoosa	Triangular savoury fried cookie
Sandsak	Co-pilot, sandbag
Sense of humour failure	Upset, angry
Shooting a cat (*braaking*)	Vomiting
Stonked	Bombed by mortars
Stroke the cat (stroking it)	Close shave, make a mistake
Takhaar	Person with long hair, hippie
The States	South Africa, home
Vasbyt	Determination (teeth clenching)
Vellies, veld skoene	Traditional farmer's shoes
Voeltjie	Junior pilot (Eng: 'little bird')
Wind your neck in	Come down to earth

Introduction

Theirs is not to make reply
Theirs is not to reason why
Theirs is but to do and die
Alfred Lord Tennyson

One of the most vivid memories I have of the bush war in South West Africa/Angola is of the sunrise. The dull red orb rises in the hazy air and casts golden fingers through the distant cumulus and over the Ovamboland plains. When it first appears on the horizon, the temperature is already in the high twenties and will rise to forty or more during the day and with the humidity close to saturation point, the atmosphere would be searing, damp and oppressive. In summer the area seems to be half mud pond and half beach sand littered with palm trees. The small lakes of water, or *shonnas*, are only a foot or so deep and are filled by the awesome afternoon thunderstorms that crash and boom, for an hour or two, and then release a torrent of water that stops all activity in its tracks. My guess is they soak into the water table that eventually feeds the massive Okavango Delta to the south-east which, to this day, is one of the most beautiful and unspoilt nature reserves in the world.

When the *shonnas* fill up in the rainy season there is a massive proliferation of wildlife. Fish that have lain asleep under the sand for six months come alive to breed and feed on billions of insects. The sky and ground become thick with bird life that feeds the predators further up the ecological ladder, in a frenzied and vicious cycle of life.

The indigenous people of the area, the Ovambo, are an integral part of the same cycle, although for them it became vicious for a different reason. For thousands of years they have fed on the wildlife and the modest fruits born of the sand. But for all its abundance to the fauna the land is not generous to the people. Winter is dry, dusty and cold, parching the land of virtually all life except the relentless invasion of flies and mosquitoes, both of which carry deadly diseases such as malaria and sleeping sickness. Summer brings rain, but there is a high price for the merciful deliverance of water, such as the suffocating heat and humidity and the insect count that increases a thousand fold. A time-honoured system of tribal customs and traditions dovetail with the landscape to give the inhabitants a primitive and modestly successful life.

Then an apex predator arrived in the form of colonial Europeans who brought with them religion, agriculture, medicine, mechanisation, clothing and many other forms of environmental control. Although life became a little easier for the locals, the white man also brought problems such as VD, alcoholism and pox. Asinine greed and bone headed bureaucracy was their trademark and they gave a little and took far too much for themselves. Unfortunately the passive nature of the Ovambo people provided little resistance to these things.

If the 20th Century in Africa is to be marked by one overriding political factor, it is the reversal of colonial rule that was established largely up to the end of the Victorian era. What the nations of Western Europe achieved with colonisation in the seventeenth, eighteenth and nineteenth centuries was effectively neutralised and often wantonly destroyed in widely publicised struggles that repulsed the rest of the world with their barbarity. The fact that the colonials were equally bloody-minded and ruthless in their acquisitions is only becoming general knowledge now. Often the "liberating" African rulers who reclaimed their national heritage were nothing more than thugs and bullies and the people ended up far worse off than before.

Although at the end of the seventies I was too young to fully appreciate the political issues and their implications, and very privileged to fly such wonderful equipment, to my mind there was always an underlying feeling of futility about the war, and as it turned out the whole exercise achieved nothing and led nowhere.

At the time, the South African government was fighting a war on two fronts. The first was basically a civil war fought within our motherland against a proliferation of black liberation movements, and the second was in South West Africa, which was a South African protectorate. To compound this nightmare was the tribal friction within each of our fourteen local tribes fighting against each other for political dominance.

Both were low intensity wars cleverly conceived by the Eastern Bloc to wear down the South African government with protracted psychological and economic attrition. The government responded to these threats with a conventional military approach, while the "liberation" movements used non-conventional or terrorist tactics. What this means is that our war was very expensive to run, while theirs cost virtually nothing. The two approaches were completely different and both devastatingly effective in their own right.

On both sides young men in the prime of their youth were sent to fight a war very few of them understood, a war that had many defeats and victories and no beginning or end. It was the war with no shape.

It is difficult to balance the end result of this war with the price that was paid by both sides. In retrospect, the monumental cost in terms of life and resources and the watery political conclusion culminated in an obvious victory for the majority of people in Southern Africa. Communism, the ghastly peril that was used to justify the war, has since collapsed and has played a minimal part in the new South Africa.

There were also less obvious consequences such as the thousands of distressed families who lost young men and women on the threshold of their adulthood, and the effects of post-traumatic stress syndrome that had far reaching effects on the victims and the people close to them.

Putting the dangers aside, from a pilot's point of view I cannot imagine a more exciting and fulfilling job for an adventurous young man. The variety of operations and the aircraft we flew, as well as the camaraderie and the opportunities created for our futures were simply unparalleled.

The helicopter crews flew with every facet of the defence force, but most of our operations were with the Reconnaissance Corps, 32 Battalion, ParaBats, the Police and Infantry, as well as the non-combatant services such as the Medical Corps and the Engineers; each benchmark organizations against which any military force in the world could be measured in those days, and it was a pleasure working with them.

The involvement of the Air Force, and in particular the helicopter squadrons, was pivotal to both the internal and external confrontations. It allowed mobility and punch far beyond anything the enemy was capable of, and the helicopter squadrons in particular were integral in every part of these engagements. The chopper aircrews received pro-rata the greatest number, and among the highest decorations of all the military units in the South African Defence Force, but it must be stressed that no single mustering can be placed above another.

This book is an attempt to capture the essence of the helicopter crews and the people involved with them, and to give the reader some idea of a SAAF chopper pilot's life in those days. The time frame is from 1973 to 1983 and is based mainly on my personal experiences, although some of the stories are a collage of events and some of the names used are fictitious.

Thank you to all my SAAF buddies and the people I met during my military career for making this book possible. I am sure every one of them could write a book like this.

1

The '*Roofie*'

Mother Earth…my life support system…

As a soldier
I must drink your blue water…
live inside your red clay and eat your green skin.

I pray my boots will always kiss your face, and
my footsteps march to your heartbeat.

Carry my body through space and time…
you are my connection to the Universe
and all that comes after.

I am yours and you are mine.
I salute you.
First Earth Battalion poem

There were thousands of us gathered in the car park of the Milpark railway station chatting to family and friends, laughing and crying, hugging and shaking hands, clinging to girlfriends and nervously telling bawdy jokes to our buddies. This was truly a cross section of white South African youth, and you could tell by the clothes we wore and our hairstyles which sector we hailed from. Some had been briefed by friends who had preceded them in the army and had short hair, practical shoes and conservative shirts and jeans, and there was even the occasional safari suit, *vellies* and matching knee length stockings indicating a more conservative background. Most of us were dressed in comfortable jeans and T-shirts with a few making a rebellious statement with psychedelic shirts, patched jeans and long hair, fags in fingers, trying desperately to look cool in very un-cool circumstances. The moms and girlfriends were in various states of despair and the dads and siblings mostly looked on in silence, some mildly concerned, but most seemingly indifferent.

Another dad was speaking to mine and I heard him say, "At last, maybe they can straighten the little bastard out!" My dad nodded knowingly, but stopped short of commenting while I was within earshot.

All around us were uniformed soldiers with "V" shaped stripes on their upper arms, called corporals and sergeants I found out later, looking out over the crowd with quiet menace like vultures eyeing their carrion.

"Quiet please," a heavily accented voice boomed over a megaphone, "would all the family and friends please move away so that we can hold a roll call. Thank you." That incidentally was the most polite thing I ever heard a corporal say in my entire military career. We said our goodbyes and finally our National Service intake stood facing the immaculate and identically uniformed Officers and NCOs. Roll call took ages, and as soon as it was concluded we got the first shock of many to come. The corporals started bellowing at us to get on the train, and for a few seconds we all just stood there in dumb disbelief, and then bolted for the carriages like panic stricken cattle. During the stampede some stumbled and fell in the rush with the odd suit case bursting open, only to have a corporal stand over them screaming abuse, but most of us just ran like hell.

As I climbed on the train I got my first dose of military bluster from one of the corporals. *"Jy gaan bakstene kak jou donnerse takhaar!"* (You're going to shit bricks you bloody hippie) he growled, referring to my long blonde locks. I could hardly speak Afrikaans but I got the message and, as it transpired, he was right. Once on the train we established our unofficial rank, *rowe* (scabs) or *roofies* (little scabs), and I had a feeling in the pit of my stomach that life was going to be very different for the next year.

The train journey was as uncomfortable as any I can remember with most of the guys staying up and chatting through the night. I value my sleep, but there was one idiot in my compartment who told stupid jokes incessantly and when I finally told him to shut up he lay there sobbing like a baby so, very reluctantly, I spent the rest of the night trying to cheer him up, which was a wasted act of charity I discovered later. Within twenty-four hours he was being smashed into the ground, as were we all, by a bunch of soulless disciplinarians called corporals. After what seemed like a lifetime of discomfort, the flat and chalky, semi-arid plains of the Northern Cape were starting to glow in the dawn, indicating we were close to Kimberley.

At the station we were again herded onto the back of a row of Bedford trucks and driven to the stores, our first call at my new home the Danie Theron Combat School, and my new unit, the 11 Commando Battalion in Kimberley. We stood in a long single file and when my turn came, I was greeted by an enormous woman, not tall but with a pronounced horizontal aspect and an expressionless round face, wearing a very loose fitting dress that was draped strategically to cover her generous body and keep her cool in the blistering heat. Balloons of fat the size of my thigh hung from the back of her arms that wobbled as she shuffled through my file checking the forms. After a while she scowled at me through her pink rimmed butterfly glasses, grunted and pivoted her bulk around with such alarming speed I feared her body would shear off at the ankles, but they handled the torque with ease. She made off to the back of the room with her dress billowing like the sails of a clipper, the floorboards creaking in her wake, returning with my file substantially thicker and pointing to the entrance of the stores.

A corporal stood in front of a row of stores clerks with huge piles of assorted kit behind them and simply shouted a number. We filed past as the numbers turned out to be what *he* thought was our uniform size, and the clerks dug into big cardboard boxes and literally threw the fresh new browns (fatigues) at us, followed by webbing, bedding, towels, underwear, you name it. Fitting our boots and stepouts (No. 1 uniform) was done with a little more care, and then a trommel with bedding and eating utensils inside was thrown at us, and finally our R1 rifles were piled on top. We stuffed everything into the trommel except the rifle. A few of us discovered the *balsak* (ball-bag), a large cylindrical canvas bag that could hold all the clothing, and by late morning we grunted and wheezed into our quarters with all this kit.

The bungalows were large school hall sized rooms that held one hundred and ten beds, more or less one company of soldiers. There were eight rows of beds with a *kas* (locker) between each bed and two small rooms which we used to store our civilian stuff. We trooped off to lunch eating out of a pressed metal pan or *varkpan* (pig pan), and I suffered my first dose of military heartburn, a truly diabolical experience brought on by a slice of beef so tough that my new boots would have made more delicate fare.

After lunch we stood in a long queue for our haircuts and this was the first real memory of the army for most blokes. The piles of hair lying on the floor were amazing and everyone was shorn to a number one brush cut. The rebellious shoulder length hair I had so carefully cultivated disappeared in a few strokes of the razor, and I was left staring at a person in the mirror that I had never seen before. Curiously we were not allowed to shave our heads bald, not that it would have made any difference, but we had to shave our faces which was a new experience for me and quite a few of the others, and this together with the sweating over the next weeks stopped my pimples in their tracks, for which I shall be eternally grateful.

The first two weeks of basic training were the toughest. I was terribly unfit and the exercise was very tough. They would break you down psychologically with the idea of re-moulding you into a soldier. If anyone in your section made a mistake the whole section was punished, usually by making you run *om die boom* (around the tree), which happened literally thousands of times.

Besides the mental and physical fatigue we were plagued by blisters on our feet, chafing between the legs and under the arms, water on the knees and the stinking summer heat, topped off with swarms of mosquitoes and flies, plus, for me, a newcomer to nature's arsenal of misery, the corn cricket or "Parktown prawn", surely the most disgusting creature on the planet. It could destroy days of cleaning and polishing by simply walking through the door and shitting all over your hard work. If you crushed it with a boot the mess was even worse, and if you kicked it you risked destroying the hard work of several other troops as well. The only workable solution was to coax it back out the door and let it go and fuck someone else around.

The exercise in the stifling summer heat was so extreme that dehydration was a big problem as well, and large numbers of pasty-faced *roofies* were carted off to the sickbay. They also put de-worming powder in the food and bluestone in the coffee and just about everyone got *gyppo guts* or diarrhoea in the first few days. Regularly someone sprinted off to the bogs, but we were so full of sweat and dirt during our training that nobody would have noticed if you crapped in your pants.

After the first few weeks everyone was tuned in and the *vasbyt* (teeth clenching) became more of a routine. We also learned the hard way where the term *rowe* came from. Our elbows and hands were covered in scabs from the cuts and grazing caused by continuous contact with the coarse desert soil. The terms *gyppo*, meaning to do as little as possible or, preferably, absolutely nothing, and *naafi*, short for "no ambition and fuck all interest", became part of our rapidly expanding army lingo.

The morning inspections were at six sharp, by which time we had already done PT and a five kilometre run, followed by a shower and breakfast and then cleaning and polishing our kit. For the first few days we made our beds neatly and tidied up, but that soon changed as the demands of the corporals became more exacting, and the punishments for non-conformance very severe. By the end of basics, the standards were so high that the beds and bedding were lined up to the millimetre with string stretched from one end of the bungalow to the other, the floor was so shiny you could see your face in it, every bit of glass and brass was gleaming and you could eat your breakfast off the shower room floor. We bit the edges of our beds to make them sharp and placed a towel at the base with our unit emblem brushed into it. Every single bed and *kas* of the one hundred and ten troops was identical, and the acid test for cleanliness was when a corporal wiped the working parts of your rifle on your bed sheets. The slightest mark and the whole section would be in big trouble. For the last few weeks of basics we slept on the floor underneath our beds because it could take hours to make them again, and we skated around on bits of cut up blanket to keep the floor shiny.

Those who did not conform suffered greatly as they got hammered by the corporals and their mates alike. A few of the guys in our bungalow decided they would be better occupied elsewhere and went AWOL. One poor bastard simply felt like driving his car, but mostly they were just homesick. The Military Police rounded them up with surprising ease and they were charged and sent off to DB, or detention barracks, at another camp in Bloemfontein if I remember correctly, and when they eventually rejoined us they all had a vacant look in their eyes and said very little; a life altering experience by all accounts. We thought we had it tough but God knows what the poor bastards went through in *die kas*. One bloke didn't like showering and battled to keep his space tidy, so he was hauled into the shower by a few of his mates and smeared with red floor polish and then scrubbed down with floor brushes. Another was caught with a beer in his kit and drilled by the corpies until he collapsed. But mostly we just ran and ran and ran for the slightest infringements, and often for no reason at all. And my goodness did we get fit and tough!

Comparatively, our time on the shooting range was a rather leisurely affair; due to the safety concerns the corporals didn't bugger us around too much. The R1 was a joy to shoot. It fired the NATO 7.62mm round that was a gassed up .308 hunting bullet and it rewarded with a good kick and accuracy. About the only thing I did when I was young to prepare for the army was shoot flies off the patio with my pellet gun and joined the shooting team at school; so the chickens came home to roost for me! After ten rounds I was nailing the bullseye every time, which drew the attention of the corporals and I was singled out with a few other guys. This was significant, because we were allowed to ride home on a Bedford while all the other one hundred odd troops ran the seven miles back to base in the rain.

We were lucky in one respect because we had a thunderstorm at least once a day, compliments of the typical summer weather, and spent some time indoors being lectured. During the last week of basics we had a written test on all the theory we had been taught. All the lectures had been in Afrikaans and the questions for the test were shouted verbally by one of the corporals, and we had to answer in Afrikaans, a noteworthy problem for me at that stage. Needless to say I got zero, the only one in our company to achieve this "distinction", although there were a few others in single digits. When I was confronted by my corporal about it I explained that I was learning Afrikaans as fast as I could, and for this I got the nickname of *fokken Engelsman* (fucking Englishman), and unfortunately it stuck! God help me if I had called one of them a 'fucking Dutchman'. I would have had my head staved in such was the mentality of some of those guys.

Our much-hyped first pass at the end of six weeks was a total anti-climax. We earned about twenty eight rand a month, and the return train fare home was, yes, twenty-eight rand, so there was nothing left for *jolling* (partying). When I got home my folks were stunned at the physical difference in me and I must say it is probably the fittest and healthiest I have ever been.

The next phase was advanced training where we were taught how to be commandos or urban warfare soldiers. This proved to be even more demanding than basics, despite being very fit at that stage. We learned riot control, soon to become a big issue in South Africa, and urban combat, plus the skills needed for normal combat, if there is such a thing. The practical phase saw us having a few hours sleep a day for about two weeks or so, doing D formation and riot control in the dead of night. Jumping off the back of moving Bedfords, and being abused by mock gangs made up of our corporals who pelted us with bottles, rocks, tear gas, smoke grenades and thunderflashes, and in one instance a piece of dog shit that took two washes to get the smell out of my browns. They also booted our food onto the ground in front of us and cut our water supply. This was exhausting in the extreme but fortunately no one cracked, and I suppose we were just so used to getting messed around that it made very little difference. The physical training also moved up a notch and we started to do pole PT which involved running with telephone poles on our shoulders, long runs with full kit, and sometimes when things got a bit rough, long runs with full kit *and* poles. One such exercise was done in a thunderstorm, and is the only time I can remember becoming completely numb. The pain, discomfort and exhaustion were so extreme that my mind simply blocked it out. But this was to toughen us up more than anything, and as soon as we had showered the hell was forgotten and we carried on as if nothing had happened.

During this phase, we had a visit by a Puma helicopter that deeply impressed me. The idea was to practice getting in and out of the chopper quickly, trooping drills in military jargon, but it was also a PR exercise to encourage recruits to join the Air Force. I was sitting on the rugby field with my section, eagerly awaiting my turn for a flip around the base when the guy next to me mumbled, "now that's a serious bit of gear". I had seen this bloke on the other side of our bungalow but never spoken to him, and I was mildly surprised to hear him speak English. "Ja, I reckon those blokes have the best job in the whole outfit." I gave this a bit of thought and decided he was right. That the Puma was singularly the most impressive aircraft I had ever seen. I watched it taking off and landing, the troops pouring in and out of the big doors, handling the load effortlessly, smelling the burning AVTUR bellowing out of the turbines and the thunder of the rotors making the ground shake, and I had one of the most inspiring and serious thoughts I can remember. I always had this notion about flying but simply hadn't a clue how to go about it. I had ten years of camps to do after my year in Kimberly, and there was little chance of any meaningful advancement in the army; there was also the question of my future and career. Older friends of mine went to great lengths to *gyppo* the camps. They disrupted your work and family life and many guys had to spend their annual leave doing combat drills or time up in South West Africa on *die grens,* or the border as it came to be known. After the flip I went over to the corporal who was taking the names down and told him I wanted to be a pilot. He smiled wryly, no doubt reflecting on my zero rating as a soldier, and said in broken English that he wouldn't trust me with an old Bedford, never mind a Puma. The only other person that put his name down was the other English guy. This was really exciting, and to be blunt, ordinarily my last career choice would have been in the military, but somehow this was different.

After twelve weeks of basics we were divided into groups for specialized training, or phase two. The main groups were drivers, light machine guns or LMGs, mortars, signals and admin/stores. Everyone wanted to be a driver which seemed like the cushiest job, and the absolute cherry was a storeman. I ended up doing signals, which turned out to be quite enjoyable.

The NCO in charge of us was a guy called Sergeant "Killer" Smith who had apparently drilled a troop to death, a hollow legend credited to many people in the army, but despite his fearsome presence and reputation he gave us a very easy time compared to the other sections. We had about a dozen different types of radios to learn about, the various frequencies and what they are used for and how they were affected by weather and atmosphere and so on. This was a massive departure from the blood, sweat and tears of basics. It was also a chance to use my so-called zero-rated brain. You may be relieved to know I passed the written test at the end of this phase.

The drivers, who everyone thought had got it made, spent most of their time cleaning the grease traps, washing trucks or pushing them around in the rain as punishment. The LMG guys had the worst time by far. Their sergeant was a maniac who kept them on the limit of their endurance and I can only imagine detention barracks being worse than what they went through. I had a notion that he really enjoyed killing people. They trained on the obsolete Vickers machine gun of First World War vintage, a fine piece of equipment but I never saw it used on the border, and the FN MAG – a Light Machine Gun that was fully up to date and a greatly admired piece of kit. We often saw them in tears, dragging their desperate asses around with poles on their shoulders and clutching the tripods and barrels of the Vickers under their arms. Later, when asked about their training under this animal, they all said he was a great guy; such is the resilience of youth. The mortars guys had a sergeant who was tough, but fair, and a stickler for cleanliness and discipline, and they came out on top when the evaluations were done. I remember him going berserk during inspection one morning when he found a speck of fly shit on a light fitting that would be invisible to a normal human. *"Fokken varkhok!"* (fucking pigsty), he screamed with his eyes bulging and his face purple, and then drilled them non-stop for hours. His troops had spent the whole weekend cleaning and polishing the room until it sparkled, only to have it destroyed by an errant fly.

After phase two we were sent to our respective sections in preparation for our border stint, but the whole atmosphere was different as we were a team and trained soldiers at that stage. We were trained, as far as the army was prepared to take us as National Servicemen, and all we lacked was operational experience.

In final preparation for going to the border we spent a week at Schmidsdrif, an area west of Kimberly that was used specifically for our border training. It had to be really tough if we were to be effective in an operational environment and this area is a moonscape of jagged rocks peppered with thorn bushes that cling tenaciously to your clothing and cut any exposed skin. Being mid winter, the temperatures were sub-zero at night balanced by a dry arid heat during the day, and as usual there was no time for rest as we practiced ambushes and combat at night and did live ammo exercises during the day. When we did get some rest we slept like babies on the frost covered rocks. One night I was standing guard with Jules, one of my buddies from basics who used to play guitar for us in the evenings. We had a lot in common and started talking about home and music, cars and bikes, and admiring nature's own lightshow, the Milky Way, as we "*naaied beat*" in the freezing cold. He was totally bi-lingual so at last I could talk in my mother tongue, but by default my Afrikaans was becoming quite fluent at that stage, even though it consisted mainly of military slang.

After returning to Kimberley it was back to the endless inspections, drilling and pole PT. But I was in for a pleasant surprise.

2

MMI

Faster, Higher, Stronger
Olympic Motto, Henri Martin Didon

About two weeks before we were due to leave for the border, I was summoned to Captain Strydom's office, and told to report to the Military Medical Institute in Pretoria for pilot selection. I had all but forgotten about my application, and found myself thoroughly looking forward to a leisurely break from our training, an excellent *gyppo.*

I caught the train and the next morning was collected at Pretoria station and taken to the Air Force Gym in Valhalla, where I felt very at home because I spent a large part of my childhood just down the road. I reported to the MMI later that morning. From the outside, the building looked like any modern office block, but inside it was like a bomb shelter, with bare grey concrete walls and ceilings, dim neon lights and freezing cold. Even in the middle of summer it was cold in that building. After having my credentials checked I was ushered into the large mess hall that had a strangely high ceiling, probably because the room was originally designed for another function, and full of metal tables and benches. It was packed with about three hundred young men, all my age and wearing a wide variety of uniforms, with a few guys dressed in civvies, all chatting loudly. I had to reflect on the difference between this place and Milpark. Here the atmosphere was one of confidence and excitement, whereas Milpark was little more than morose foreboding.

Soon an attractive young female lieutenant stood up on a chair and we hushed while she divided us into groups of twenty, and told us briefly how the selection process worked.

I picked up a large manila envelope with my name and number on it at the door and made my way to the Psychology Department, that was housed in some pre-fabricated buildings outside. The tests were dead simple and when we were finished there was a lingering suspicion that they were not IQ tests, but an investigation into the less obvious workings of our minds. This was followed by an interview with one of the psychiatrists where they asked some very probing questions about family, friends, drugs, sex etc. This whole process was quite new and spooky to me, and I left the room feeling quite bewildered. A short while later we were dozing outside in the winter sun when four names including mine were read out, and we were told to wait in the mess hall. I never saw the other sixteen guys in my group again.

The next morning, the mess had few more than an hundred guys in it, and it was very clear that the SAAF was quite specific about whom it wished to fly its aircraft. Considering it was taxpayer's money and the gargantuan cost of the equipment and training, I guess they had every right to be fussy. On that basis, I decided it was a privilege to be there, and this was an opportunity that had to be grabbed with both hands. They owed me nothing.

The tests continued for the next week. Not only was every single facet of our physical being evaluated, but we were constantly under scrutiny. Any anomalies in behaviour such as sulkiness, complaining, bad temper, belligerence, shyness, even to the way you dressed and carried yourself, were all thoughtfully noted by the nurses and doctors in the manila envelope that we had to carry everywhere, but were not allowed to open. And the guys fell like flies. Decompression, eyes, ears, nose and throat, co-ordination, EEG, ECG, a whole string of eye tests, disorientation and on and on, and always the queue for the next test got shorter and shorter.

At the end of the medicals, the group had thinned to about forty guys and we only had one more obstacle: the selection board.

The selection board consisted of a panel of senior pilot training officers, one of the MMI doctors and someone from the Chief of Staff's office. I had spent the whole of the previous evening ironing my army stepouts and polishing the badges, and I stood outside the interview room (I didn't want to crease my pants), as we were called in one by one. The interview lasted about fifteen minutes and when it was over the applicant was told to leave immediately, so there was no way of gleaning any tips from them.

A while after the process had started someone pitched up late and excused himself to the second lieutenant in charge with a sheepish grin on his face,

"Sorry I'm late lieutenant, but I … ."

"Well, you can fuck off."

"But how can you say that?" he whined, starting to blush.

"You're supposed to be here *before* eight."

"You're only a Lieutie, let me speak to … " brimming with indignation.

"Heeelloooo" he bellowed, rapping his knuckles on the desk, "this is reality, not fucking baboon land! Come back when you get your priorities right." After surviving the medical selection against incredible odds, he blew it by arriving late on the last day.

Eventually my name was called and I went into the room feeling as if my mind and body were detached. My movements were mechanical but my mind was racing, and it was probably the most nervous I have ever been for an interview. The panel sat behind a line of steel tables piled with files and notepads, in front of them a lone wooden chair that seemed abnormally small. I sat down at their invitation. They were all smiling and relaxed, and although they were in full blues with more brass than I had ever seen in one place, somehow there was not the same military rigidity I experienced with my seniors in the army. Although Afrikaans, the colonel in charge spoke to me in immaculate English. After a few questions, I was asked to motivate my reasons for wanting to fly, and I recounted my model building as a child, building my own kites and being fascinated by the aircraft flying around where we lived in Valhalla. I put on the table what I had, as modest as it was, and avoided the romance. In an amazing stroke of luck I was asked to describe how a radio worked in Afrikaans. A few months earlier this would have been my undoing, but I flew through it and noticed them nodding their heads enthusiastically, almost willing me on. Finally, they thanked me for my interest in the SAAF, and I in turn thanked them and excused myself politely, snapping them a sharp army salute in the process.

As I closed the door behind me, I looked around at the faces of the remaining guys staring anxiously at me, and I felt truly sorry for the poor bastards. I just knew I was in, and I had never been more chuffed in my life.

3
Sifuma Ops

"... for they do not sleep by day or by night"
Apophis

Back in Kimberley we spent the last few days getting our kit ready for our time at the border. Most of the terrorist activity in those days was in the Caprivi Strip, a finger of land that points east from the top of South West Africa, with Angola and Zambia on the northern side and Botswana to the south. There was a line of small army camps that spread along the Caprivi with the army headquarters at Katima Mulilo on the eastern end. Near here the Caprivi comes to a point at a place called Mpalela Island, which is the confluence of the Chobe River that flows in from Botswana and the mighty Zambezi River that flows in from Zambia.

We were sent to a camp at the point where the borders of Angola, Zambia and the Caprivi meet called Sifuma, which means "place of the elephant". Because of the war, there was no hunting and more importantly no poaching of wildlife in the area.

A C160 Transall flew us from Kimberley to Mpacha and from there we drove on sand roads to a camp called Kwando where we spent the first night. I did my beat after sunset with one of the *oumanne* (old boys) in the camp and then climbed into my sleeping bag in a 16 x 16 tent. I had been asleep for a short while when all hell broke loose. The base erupted with rifle fire, mortars, flares, FN MAGs and .50 calibre Brownings. We had been briefed earlier what to do if we got attacked, so I leapt out of the tent and ran to my place on the wall, where I started shooting into my designated arc of fire. I was more bewildered than scared, something was not right, and sure enough a siren went off and the whole thing stopped as quickly as it had started. It was a drill contrived to scare the shit out of us *roofies*, and it worked to a large extent giving us our first real taste of the bush war. There were two casualties in our section; one bloke had skinned his shins on a guy rope and the other had soiled himself in his sleeping bag.

The next morning we left for Sifuma, our home for the next three months, and arrived at about lunchtime. It was positioned right on the cutline dividing the Caprivi and Angola in relatively thick bush, with no fences or power lines for hundreds of kilometres. The roads were little more than soft sand tracks, churned up by military vehicles and the rain.

Communication was by long wave radio, choppers were used for emergencies (they were on call at Mpacha) and two very well worn Bedford trucks provided the transport. They had been landmine proofed by piling sandbags onto the tray at the back and cutting the roof off the cab. Traversing the sandy terrain with the weight of the sandbags, plus a section of troops with kit, was way beyond the capabilities of these old bangers and we had endless problems with reliability. Surviving a land mine explosion in them would have been strictly in the hands of the Good Lord. The only vehicle that handled these conditions with any competence was the Hyena anti-landmine vehicle with an angular armour plated body mounted on an F250 chassis, it looked strangely like its namesake, and was the only convincing attempt at solving this potentially catastrophic problem that I saw during my National Service. It was a predecessor to the Buffel which became a military benchmark for this type of vehicle. Unfortunately it could only carry nine people including the driver, and because it always travelled in front of the Bedfords, and consequently got blown up first, it was probably safer on the Bedfords.

The camp was pleasant although very basic and functional in the extreme. It comprised of four sand walls called revetments, about eight feet high that surrounded a rash of 16 x 16 tents. Walls of sandbags protected sensitive areas like the fuel dump, generators, ops room, sickbay and the outlook posts on each corner of the camp, and the more permanent structures were made out of logs chopped from the surrounding bush. A diesel generator droned all day until ten at night, supplying electricity to essentials like the ops room, sickbay and workshop. There was one light bulb in each tent, and mercifully we had proper beds to sleep on, and plenty of water as the Kwando River was only a few hundred metres away.

The whole area from south-eastern Angola through the Caprivi Strip to the Okavango Delta in the south was teeming with wildlife. This area is now a popular tourist destination with Sifuma an information centre and game viewing boats on the Kwando etc. Visitors frequently comment on the large amount of military debris lying around in the bush, and it's reasonable to suspect that a few unexploded land mines and mortar bombs still litter the area. But the bush is still unspoilt and is a charming example of how Africa used to be.

The local bushmen still used sleds that they dragged through the soft sand and lived as they have for many thousands of years. We did a tour around the local kraals with a doctor one day and a bushman tried to sell us a python skin that was the length of the Bedford. It must have been an incredible reptile when it was alive. He wanted five rand for it, which we thought was outrageously expensive, even if we had been allowed to buy skins. Even in those days there were strict conservation laws in place and a good thing too, as you can imagine how long the game would have lasted with an army occupying the area.

On one of our patrols we came across a path through the bush a few hundred metres wide that looked as if a giant steamroller had lumbered out of control and flattened everything as it smashed its way for kilometres into the distance. A herd of elephants a few hundred strong had pulled every tree and bush over in an impressive display of brute strength. Something had upset them; maybe it was mating season, or one of them had died, or maybe even a thunderstorm. I wonder if a herd that size still exists anywhere in Africa, but with the endless political turmoil that decays the protection structures for these animals, as well as corrupt bureaucrats and poachers that enjoy an orgiastic fest of wildlife murder for profit, I very much doubt it.

There had not been any notable terrorist activity in this area for years as the main thrust of incursions had shifted west to the area between Buffalo and Ruacana called Owamboland, where there was a substantial local population to exploit and reasonably good roads that made access from their bases in Angola easier.

The Portuguese Army was still in attendance to the north of us at a base called Luiana, also next to the Kwando River on the Angolan side. They were known to have ongoing problems with landmines, so the area was still active and we were warned repeatedly not to drop our guard.

We had a few interesting encounters with them. They arrived one day to buy some diesel from us with a sable antelope that they had shot on the way. We mounted its impressive horns outside our pub and had fresh meat and biltong for a while. Their attitude was very different from ours, having a much more casual approach to the war. They endured three uninterrupted years in the bush and had been really hammered by the enemy in the past, so their *gatvol* (indifferent) attitude was understandable.

We were invited to visit their base and our section was chosen for the trip. We set out one morning in the Hyena and a Bedford, and predictably the Bedford broke down in a river in the middle of nowhere. Being the radio operator, I called Sifuma and they in turn called the Portuguese who sent out one of their trucks to collect the stranded troops. In a rare display of camaraderie our seniors decided to stay with the troops in the stricken Bedford, and we continued in the Hyena and arrived at Luiana in good time. We were greeted by their commanding officer and senior staff who mistakenly took us for senior ranks as we were not wearing rank. For some strange reason they thought I was the commanding officer of our camp, which surprised me because although I was nineteen, I looked about fifteen. Their own commanding officer was a very dignified looking middle aged man who pumped my hand and slapped me on the back enthusiastically, led me into their mess and sat me down at the head of the table with a large plate of prawns and a bottle of chilled rose' wine. The language barrier prevented the disgust of my travel mates from being expressed as they sat under a tree with an urn of warm orange juice and a *mielie* each. I got on like a house on fire with their boss, although neither of us had a clue what the other was talking about, and by the time our dignitaries arrived, I had demolished the fare and was quite pickled from the wine. The severe reprimand I got from our captain was wasted because I had enjoyed the best damn meal I could ever remember having in the army. In the army if you don't take it you lose it.

Later their commanding officer, Pedro (he called me 'Niiquey'), who had clearly taken a shine to me and was not at all bothered that I was a culinary impostor, had left our stuffy and aloof captain with his second in charge. He showed me around the camp that consisted of all the same elements as ours but a lot lower key. They did not bother with lookouts and patrols and their weapons were badly maintained, if at all. He showed me a line of old trucks that had been blown up by landmines and I noticed that a few of his troops were limping and badly scarred; all very disturbing. Jules traded a shirt for a beautifully made bone-handled army issue knife, and I got some camo uniform from Pedro as a thank-you present for the *gasóleo.* At one point we came across a hole the size of a swimming pool that was supposed to be a mortar pit, but with no mortar in evidence. He shouted to one of his troops who leapt into the pit and, after digging around a bit, eventually lifted an 81mm mortar out of the sand. He shook the sand out of the barrel and set it up on its stand. Another troop arrived with some bombs which the two of them proceeded to blast into

Zambia on the other side of the river, totally indifferent to where they landed or who was on the receiving end. Another noteworthy feature of the camp was the *dagga* plantation mixed in between the *mielies*, which seemed to be as important as the staple diet itself. One way or another, those guys just wanted to get out of there. Sure enough within a year of our visit they were withdrawn. Sadly, most of them had nothing to go home to, as is often the case with soldiers after a war, and many of them were physically and mentally damaged beyond redemption.

We left Luiana mid-afternoon and made our way back to Sifuma along the banks of the magnificent Kwando River, with the Hyena in front and the Portuguese truck loaded up with our troops, towing the Bedford behind. Relations with them were very cordial after that.

❖❖

Finding your boots in the pitch darkness of the tent involved fumbling under the bed and shaking them vigorously in case a scorpion or snake had moved in during the night. My rifle was a different story; I knew instinctively where that was. It had become as close to me as one of my own limbs. A few hot beers (the fridge had run out of paraffin) and playing guitar with Jules was enough to give me a mild headache, and I had only slept for three hours, having finished my beat at two. The other guys in the tent were rustling around in near silence, and one by one we made our way out to our stand-to positions on the camp's perimeter. Most of the troops had blankets over their heads, as the sharp pre-dawn chill was enough to make your eyes water and burn the membranes in your nose. They looked like black ghosts floating across the sand.

At the perimeter I rested my R1 on top of the log wall that surrounded the camp and stared out at the thick black bush into my arc of fire. The other side of the wall was a steep bank of sand that flattened out for about twenty metres before the perimeter fence, a four-metre high tangle of barbed wire reminiscent of a Second World War prison camp. The bush on the other side was chopped away just enough to allow a truck to pass.

Everyone in the camp stood there in total silence as the sky to the east began to glow a gentle silver blue, and the bush in front of me slowly started to take form. Animals and birds were grunting and chattering noisily. The air was dead still with clouds of dust hanging in patches over the treetops where the wildlife had hunted and fought for survival during the night.

Looking along the wall at the row of figures peering into the dark, I was struck by how different the guys in my section were, and yet how close we had become. Smitty was quite feisty, and fancied himself as a bit of a Rambo. Dreyer was the accident-prone youngster, almost child-like and in need of constant attention, which he got in account of the weaponry he had access to. We called him *natdroom* because of his dozy manner and his total inability to drink (he was *dronk verdriet* after two beers) and he always seemed to be a few steps behind the rest of us. *Vuilzyl* or van Zyl was so lazy he hardly ever washed himself or his uniform and had a face full of pimples and blackheads. Although kindly in manner, physically he was repulsive. I was damn pleased he did not sleep in my tent and made a conscious effort to stay upwind of him on patrol. Our Corporals Buis and Stander were the section leaders. Buis was trained at NCOs school and was a bit aloof and indifferent to the rest of us, but he was fair and did not jerk us around too much. Stander was very laid back and fatherly. Seldom without a fag in his fingers and a smile on his face, he was very popular and often called upon to keep the peace when personalities clashed. He was also an excellent shot, and I had seen him drop an impala at two hundred metres a few times. I had the dubious pleasure of gutting one of them, and discovered he had shot it clean through the heart! Jules was my buddy and we shared a love of music, often playing our guitars together in our spare time. Although we always had a good laugh at the army and the associated bullshit, he was a fine soldier. He trained hard in Kimberley, never looked for a short cut, and despite his tongue in cheek attitude I think he really enjoyed army life.

Freddie and Wayne were like Siamese twins. They were completely different in looks and personality; Freddie was tall and thin and very placid while Wayne was short, stocky and very punchy, and they were never seen apart. There were some nasty rumours of buggery between them, but these persisted without evidence. Taking up an issue with either of them was difficult as you had to deal with two accomplished bullshitters, and they covered each other's tracks with elaborate skill. This was highlighted when Freddie consistently shot full scores on the shooting range and earned a gold marksman's badge. By coincidence Wayne was always in the target trench counting the scores. Only after we got to the border did we discover Freddie was no better than any of us with the R1. Blake and Tanner were typically quiet and totally disinterested in the army. They just did their duty and never made waves, hardly bothering to make friends with anyone, and doing the absolute minimum to get by. Van

(van der Merwe) was the camp's medic but he did his patrols with our section. He was quiet and intelligent and destined to be a professional of some sort. Blake and Tanner carried the MAG LMG and under the direction of Stander wielded its awesome power. It rattled out seven hundred rounds a minute non-stop until all the ammo belts were finished and when fired at night, the barrel glowed orange-red and took a full hour to cool down.

The thirteenth member of the section was a local Bushman called Tande (teeth), whose missing front teeth earned him enormous respect as the local tribal leader. His teeth were removed deliberately in a ceremony to identify his elevated station in life, much as ceremonial tattoos or scarring would in other tribal societies. He was invaluable to our section, as without him we would have wondered aimlessly around the bush, tangling with dangerous wildlife and never having a clue about enemy activity. His village was allowed one wild animal a week for food, and because of this Stander and a few other select members in the camp occasionally shot an antelope and very rarely a giraffe or a buffalo. Other than this, hunting was prohibited.

The increasing light took the edge off the chill and Sifuma camp started to take form. The neat rows of olive green tents around the inner perimeter of sand and log revetments were faded and sagging with old age and peppered with shrapnel holes made, not by the enemy, but by careless troops who occasionally fired mortars vertically and forgot about them, or shot themselves or their buddies by mistake. Accidental discharges were taken very seriously and were probably the biggest cause of casualties.

Stand-to was done at dawn and dusk when the camp was considered most vulnerable to attack and lasted about half an hour. Once the sun appeared on the horizon there was enough light to see about fifty metres into the bush. In the distance a generator would crank noisily and splutter into life before settling into a steady drone, and this signalled the end of stand-to and we made our way back to the tents to get ready for breakfast. This normally consisted of an egg and a rasher of bacon on a slice of white bread with a mug of heartburn inducing orange juice, or ground coffee laced with bluestone, which neutralized our sexual urges. Not that there was much to get excited about in that place.

Our section was going to spend the next three days on patrol. Breakfast that morning was a particularly bland helping of scrambled eggs made from powder with a mug of water, a sure sign rations were getting low. I sometimes think we would rather have slept in the bush and eaten the crap in the rat-packs than stay in camp. Rations were collected once a week from Katima, and thinned out quickly after a few days until there was just about nothing left. A lot of the dry rations were stolen by the troops and swapped for smokes and beers in much the same way as prisoners would, so on the last day or two we always ended up eating rat-packs anyway. It's amazing that sipping on a tin of stolen condensed milk, when you were pushing beat at two in the morning, could be so rewarding.

❖❖

Sergeant Sunday was a man never to be crossed. His huge muscular frame was topped by an angular raptor-like face, with hooded eyes that missed nothing. He was a totally uncompromising disciplinarian who led from the front and by example, and I would have followed him into combat without a second thought. I had seen him reduce many a wayward troop to a snivelling wreck within minutes. Apart from his awesome presence he was very fair and showed unusual compassion for his troops when they had personal problems. As second in charge of the base, he took his orders from Captain Strydom who seldom lowered himself to speak to a troop, so most of the communication with us was left to Sunday. The combination of fear and respect we had for him meant he seldom even had to raise his voice to be obeyed to the letter. We had spent the previous month training under him. He had made damn sure we were ready for border duty, and he aimed to take every one of us home in one piece. To his credit no one had yet been injured despite some of the crazy things we did.

There was no doubt we needed discipline. Although we were very well-trained, our average age was just nineteen and the camp was bristling with arms that had to be ready to fire at all times. The risk of someone getting hurt or worse was always present. For example, our R1 rifles were modified before we left Kimberley to shoot on automatic, as well as having three different types of machine guns at our disposal: the treacherous Bren, a modified Second World War weapon prone to firing without warning, the FN MAG LMG which was similar to the Bren but totally modern, and the outstanding .50 cal Browning one of which was mounted on each corner of the camp. There were also mortars, mines, flares and grenades for all occasions, as well as diesel, petrol, AVTUR fuel for visiting choppers, gas and paraffin for the kitchen. Yet by far the most dangerous chemical in the camp was testosterone.

❖❖

The first few weeks at Sifuma were a period of adjustment. We got six hours sleep a day, there was a constant shortage of wet rations and we walked patrols for three days out of every nine, but it all settled into a routine and after a while we just took it for granted.

One morning after breakfast our section was standing in front of the ops room getting ready to depart on another patrol. We were *oumanne* by now, and there were elements of complacency beginning to lower the standards, which pissed Sunday off no end. He had seen it many times before.

"Stand in a straight stripe!" Sunday appeared out of his tent suddenly. I'm sure he'd been watching us from the darkness and had spotted a few problems already. He pulled the bayonet out of Smitty's backpack and looked with disgust at the dust stuck on the blade, and then slowly wiped each side of the blade on Smittys' cheeks while staring deep into his eyes. Watching Smitty taking the heat was great because he fancied himself as being a bit gung-ho. "Next time I'll use it to cut your balls off. See me when you get back from patrol." Visibly shaken, Smitty just stood there wide-eyed and pale with a dark streak on each cheek. He pulled my bayonet out next, but I knew it was clean. During basics a corporal had wiped my dirty bayonet on my bed sheets before inspection one day, and the whole platoon had been drilled into the ground because of it. Never again!

"Open your rifles." he barked at the rest of us. Mine was clean but I stared down the barrel to make sure. One speck of dust, referred to as "a Bedford in your barrel," and I would end up dragging a tyre around the camp with Smitty, but the mirror-like finish of the rifling was spotless. "Show me your battery." He meant the spare I carried for the radio. I felt the pocket on my backpack to make sure. As the section signaller I carried the radio on my chest, a bulky thing about the size of two shoe boxes, which was great because it sort of balanced the weight of my backpack, and if I positioned my rifle carefully I could walk for hours quite comfortably.

One by one he checked the rifles, then the magazines and kit, and finally sent Blake back to his tent to change because of a torn sleeve, probably hooked on a thorn bush somewhere. I suspected Sunday had the most dapper troops on the border.

As we walked through the camp gate we took up a large 'Y' formation with Jules and Smitty leading from the two forward points. Behind them Tande and Buis walked together, with me behind Buis and the rest of the guys following me and Stander, Blake and Tanner at the rear carrying the MAG LMG. The whole formation spread over a hundred metres or so, and opened and closed like a spring depending on the terrain and density of the bush. We stood still for a while as Sunday peered at us from the corner lookout post, with one hand resting on the .50 Browning and the other on the sandbags, he looked rather 'Napoleonic'. He gave a nod of approval and we moved off down the road towards the river.

The pace was brisk and the heat was already beating down although it was only eight o'clock. Once outside the perimeter fence we moved off the road and into the tree line, where our camouflage was better and we could see the road clearly on the one side and into the bush on the other. As we approached the river we veered north along the top of a low ridge and I noticed the shimmering of the blue Kwando River. There was no road, only old tracks that criss-crossed along the banks where four wheel drive vehicles had passed long before. When the storms started in spring, elephant grass would cover them and the whole region would become pristine African grazing for massive herds of wild animals. This river fed into the Chobe Delta to the south and because of the war, there had been almost no hunting or poaching for many years so the game density was high. It crossed my mind that, just a few months before, I was a pimply teenager who had grown up in the big smoke of Johannesburg and the only animals I'd ever seen were in a zoo. Now I was living with them in the wild.

After two hours we were hot, sweaty and dusty, so we rested up under a giant marula tree for a smoke break. Although the ground was basically beach sand, it was reasonably firm to walk on and only got soft where vehicles had been churning their way between the trees and over the flat savannah. So the patrols were not too tough on the legs. With water and rat-packs we could last like this for weeks if we had to, and arrive back at camp hardly even fatigued, again a credit to our fitness and training. Occasionally we had visiting officers who came on patrol with us to make sure we were up to scratch, but they never lasted more than half a day before they were gasping for breath, drenched in sweat and their knees wobbling. I would radio back to base that the patrol inspection was complete, and we would wait patiently for them to be collected with the Hyena.

We walked roughly northwards parallel to the river and there was no sign of any human activity. There was plenty of wildlife, mainly small herds of antelope or wildebeest and zebras. It was very hot and the air dead still. The big cats and hyenas would be dozing in the shade waiting for the coolness of nightfall, and in the distance vultures were circling in the high thermals waiting for a carcass to ravage.

After our lunch break, things slowed down noticeably. The guys were getting tired and despite threats from Buis, we started talking amongst ourselves while we were walking, a big no-no. There was a general sigh of relief when Tande turned the patrol toward the river and we then knew it would only be another hour before we got to the crocodile hole, our resting place for the night.

Once clear of the tree line we moved across a long, flat grassland or *shonna*, and again the river came into view. The bush here was green and dense, and I could not help thinking what a great place this would be for a holiday; a pristine African paradise, totally unspoilt by man and teeming with wildlife, pretty much as it had been hundreds or even thousands of years ago.

The bank of the river dropped sharply a few metres onto a sandy beach that met the water with thick patches of reeds. This was a favourite spot for crocs as they lay on the beach and sunbathed to keep their body temperature up, or in the reeds waiting to ambush unwary prey that visited the water's edge to drink. The reeds were alive with small birds chirping playfully.

As the crocodile hole came into view through the trees ahead, our mood lifted. It looked like a lake connected to the river by a wide channel and the bank dropped vertically two metres into the crystal clear water. A short distance away from the camp, a beach formed where crocodiles sunbathed next to the reeds and formed a sandy border between the *shonna* and the river that was a good few kilometres long. The river was still as a mirror, black and deep and menacing. We stood mesmerized by a fish eagle as it swooped gracefully and plucked a fish out of the river with its talons spread, leaving a shower of liquid crystals trailing behind. As we got near to the camp area, Tande moved cautiously around the outer perimeter looking for any signs of activity. It was the kind of place that the gooks would lay anti-personnel mines, but there were just hyena spoor and the serpentine lines left by a large snake in the sand.

This was a temporary camp that had been used many times over the years, and it was littered with fire ash and rusty tins from rat-packs that had been buried by the troops and then dug up by the scavenging hyenas. The perimeter was a rough semi-circle with strategically placed trenches and the riverbank formed the base. The shallow trenches gave us cover in case there was any shooting and were also quite comfortable to sleep in.

We settled in quickly and Buis sent Stander and Vuilzyl onto a low mound to stand beat because they did not like swimming. While the rest of us stripped off, Jules threw a hand grenade into the water that exploded with a muffled thump and gave off a cloud of bubbles. A dead fish floated to the surface, and we all cheered, congratulating him on his fishing skills. No self-respecting croc could handle that sort of abuse and we were able to swim in relative safety for about fifteen minutes. I jumped into the surprisingly cold water and let myself float downwards for a few seconds without touching the bottom. Escaping the dust, sweat and flies was a great feeling but suddenly I got this eerie sensation that we were being watched. Spooked, I came to the surface and I stayed there splashing around with the other guys for a few minutes feeling quite unsettled.

After the swim we just lay around the camp chatting and nibbling the bits and pieces from the rat-packs, Jules making a cup of instant coffee with condensed milk that was absolutely delicious, given the circumstances.

Tande was staring out over the *shonna* to the west chewing thoughtfully on a grass stalk. It must have been lonely for him being so completely different to us, and only being able to communicate with hand signs and a few words of broken Afrikaans.

Before the sunset, it was time for the smokers to enjoy their last smoke of the day, and we took up our positions for stand-to and arranged the beat for the night. Smoking and talking at night was forbidden and damn dangerous, and any movement was strictly limited.

Buis organized the beat with Freddie and Wayne first until ten, and then Jules and me until twelve. At about seven we all stared out over the dusty grass of the *shonna* as the sun set in a glorious blaze of orange, pale blue and indigo, and the chill of the night started to settle in. In the distance, a pack of hyenas cackled in anticipation of the night's scavenging and a pod of hippos grunted behind us in the river. I shuffled around in my sleeping bag until the sand in the trench took the shape of my body. The instant I put my head down, I was fast asleep.

❖❖

"Hey *Engelsman*, wake up." I felt Freddie nudging me gently and I was instantly wide-awake. Freddie moved off silently to his sleeping bag and I stretched over to Jules and shook his shoulder. There was obviously nothing to report, and looking over the *shonna* the only thing I could make out was the contrast in colour between the lightness of the grass and the pitch darkness of the trees on the far side. Above the trees, the millions of stars were surprisingly bright, and the only source of light. Suddenly, in the distance, a baboon screamed in terror as it succumbed, probably to a leopard. I felt shivers run down my spine, and a few of the guys shuffled in their sleeping bags but they quickly sank back into a deep slumber.

"I hate those fucking things," Jules whispered and I was not sure which animal he was talking about. Hyenas were the ones that gave me the creeps as they could get very close, always pushing their luck and totally unpredictable. I had an ingrained fear that one was going to take a snap at my face while I was sleeping. Fortunately, their cowardly nature and fear of humans kept them away most of the time.

What always amazed me about standing beat out there was the experience of absolute timelessness. You could stare into the night for ages and when you looked at your watch, five minutes would have passed, and then the next hour seemed to pass in a tick. Sometimes time passed so quickly, you wondered if you had been sleeping without realizing it.

Suddenly, Jules and I both jumped as the trees on the other side of the *shonna* came alive. A large herd of impala bolted out onto the flat grassland and headed away parallel to the river, leaving a cloud of dust hanging in the air. Something had spooked them, but had not followed them into the open, probably hyenas, too clever to waste energy chasing them, but using the trees as cover to stalk them.

My adrenalin was pumping, and my heart was thumping so loud I could hear it clearly. We looked at each other. I couldn't see his features but I knew he was grinning, wondering if I had shit myself as much as he had. We started to relax and time drifted on and on, and the only notable difference was the dust slowly settling back onto the grass.

Behind us in the camp I heard the sound of a sleeping bag zip and Blake came quietly up behind us. "I'm going for a slash," he whispered, and moved slowly into the trees to our right.

I checked my trusty old Rotary watch, we had about ten minutes of our beat to go. I noticed a soft pulse of light like distant lightning above the tree line quite far away, then three more in quick succession, followed by the soft rolling of thunder a few seconds later. This was weird because there were no clouds, nor any weather at all for that matter. I could see Jules shuffling uneasily. He moved his head at an angle to the point over the trees because peripheral vision is better at night, and I did the same, but there was no clue. There were no native settlements in that area, and almost no human activity, and although you could see a match being lit miles away in that darkness, those lights were too far away.

The bush around us was eerily quiet, as if all the wild life had stopped, listening intently and trying to figure out what was going on as well. Only the trickle of Blake peeing a few metres away could be heard.

A sharp whoosh, a huge bang and flash of light hit the *shonna*. Shrapnel tore into the trees above us showering us with twigs and leaves. The guys were struggling and cursing as they kicked their sleeping bags free, and I could hear the rifles clicking onto automatic. I was absolutely stunned and totally confused. And then I remembered Blake. "Don't shoot, don't shoot!" I screamed and luckily they listened. There was another explosion, much closer, and then two more in quick succession. Dust, sand and wood splinters blasted through the camp in a violent swirling cloud, followed by another shower of leaves. I had sand in my eyes and mouth and my ears were ringing like hell. Around us birds and bats were erupting from the bush, flapping and squealing frantically.

We were being stonked I realized with terror. The force of the mortars exploding was unbelievable and I felt totally exposed, just waiting to be blasted. Then things settled down a bit, and I wondered if anyone had been hit.

"Troops number!!" Buis shouted in a shaky voice. I found this very reassuring – at least he was okay. We numbered off one by one, all except Blake. "Blake, answer me!" Buis shouted with a mixture of fear and anger. "Answer me for fuck sake!" He choked. There was no reply.

"I'll get him." I could not believe Jules was crazy enough to get up. He moved quickly behind the line of troops to the right, and then into the trees. I could just hear him talking above the ringing in my ears. I heard Blake moan loudly, and after a short while Jules emerged out of the bush with Blake draped over his shoulders. He put him down gently next to me, and in the darkness I could just make out a large patch of blood around his abdomen. He was gasping for air and his body was rigid with pain.

Van, our medic crawled up to him and peered at the wound. "I need some light," he mumbled shakily.

"No light! Cover the wound and give him a shot of morphine. Get ready to move out. *Engelsman*, get on the radio." Buis was in charge, no doubt about that.

Something in his voice made our training kick in as we all moved simultaneously, pulling on our ammo webbing and leaving our backpacks and sleeping bags behind. We wouldn't need them now.

Behind me I could hear someone sobbing, and it seemed like we had another wounded. I made out Stander kneeling next to one of the trenches trying to pull the bloke onto his feet. "*Vasbyt* Dreyer, it's okay … come on my buddy." It was *Natdroom*, the youngster who had gone *bossies* but was otherwise unhurt.

"*Bly stil, jou doos!*" Buis was less understanding. "Shut up or I'll stick my rifle up your arse!"

"I'll look after him, just leave him alone." Stander, always the father figure, had got him up and was putting his webbing on. Buis and Stander were often at odds, but this time I was on Buis' side. The temporary camp was in a state of frenzied activity. Out of the corner of my eye, I saw flashes behind the trees in the distance again. My heart jumped and someone shouted "Here they come again!" The reaction from the troops was startling. About five guys and the MAG LMG let rip towards the flashes, but it was a waste of ammo – the flashes were a couple of kilometres away.

"Get behind the bank!" Buis shouted, and we all knew what he meant. About twenty metres away the riverbank dropped onto the sandy beach that ran next to the water. "The fucking bastards are watching us!"

Buis and Smitty carried Blake, with Stander dragging Dreyer by his webbing. In a few seconds we were all behind the bank, walking quickly in the loose sand. Tande was waving his arms and hissing through the gap in his teeth, showing us not to bunch up. Our training and discipline clicked in again, and we spread out evenly, crouching slightly to keep behind the bank, occasionally looking out across the *shonna*. This made us very difficult targets to shoot at – that is if we could be seen.

Behind us, the next salvo of mortars slammed into the camp we had occupied a few seconds before, exploding with bright flashes and blasting huge clouds of sand and debris into the air. If we had stayed, a few of us would have copped it for sure.

About two hundred metres down the beach we stopped and Buis came over to me to talk on the radio. While we were walking, I had spoken to Marais the ops clerk at Sifuma, and he had run off to call Sunday and Captain Strydom.

"What do you mean mortars?" Sunday's voice crackled in disbelief. "How bad is Blake?"

They nattered on for a while and I was getting increasingly nervous about stopping for so long, although it had only been a minute or two.

"I'll call a casevac chopper for Blake, and I want you to set an ambush. Get Tande to try and move you behind them, but make sure you don't get jumped. I'll bring a section out at first light. *Pasop julle*!" (be careful)

As we moved off, the creepy notion we were being watched returned again, but this time it meant something. We walked for half an hour or so, my legs aching from the soft river sand. It was my turn to carry Blake with Jules and I was shocked at how limp his body had become and how he was drenched in sweat and blood. He could hardly move his feet and moaned gently, but the morphine would have had a good grip on him. It was really hard going, but I didn't mind. I finally understood why the training was so damn tough. Dreyer was fine now, following Stander like a puppy, and I kind of felt sorry for him. None of us knew we were going to hit that shit, and it affected all of us differently.

At last we stopped on the southern point of the *shonna* where the water drained into the river in summer, and although it was almost pitch dark, we could see the entire length right up to the crocodile hole about two kilometres away. Buis came up to me and whispered into the microphone, and I could hear Marais on the other end saying the Puma was airborne from Mpacha and would be with us in twenty minutes or so. I changed the radio channel to speak to the pilots. There was no answer so they were still out of range, but I was not surprised as these old A20 radios were never very good at the best of times.

Van was getting very worried about Blake. He was talking to him softly trying to keep him conscious but I could hear the tension in his voice. Blake's breathing was very shallow. He had stopped moaning, and for the first time since I had known him, I really felt something for the guy. He had paid a high price for a piss. But at least he was going home and somehow I felt he would be okay once he was on the chopper. But this business was far from over and the thought of more of us being airlifted out, sent a chill down my spine.

We sat in dead silence until the distant drone of the approaching chopper broke the stillness.

"Charlie section this is Jumbo 5, do you copy?" the pilot's voice crackled over the radio.

"Jumbo 5 we copy you, stand by for white phos," I answered. We had moved into a large semi-circle around the tree line with Buis, Blake and Stander at the centre roughly where the chopper would land. The chopper intercepted the river a few kilometres away and turned to follow the line of the bank.

Jules threw the phos grenade onto the *shonna* and it exploded with a soft thump and a shower of white light. The thick white smoke hung in the air and soon the Puma was coming up behind us with its landing light playing on Stander who was now standing up waving his arms. As it touched down the plume of grenade smoke swirled in an arched vortex through the blades and a massive cloud of dust billowed up taking its place. The door slid open and a few guys jumped out with a stretcher. In seconds Blake was on board, the door closed, and the big machine was lifting off and turning back over the river, perfectly camouflaged in the dark except for the sound of the beating rotors and hissing turbines.

We had to move again, we made good progress without the burden of having to carry Blake. Tande led us along the tree line for a few hundred metres and then cut into the bush. It was pitch black, and most of our orientation was done by sound alone. By now I was getting very tired and my nerves were raw. Every snapped twig and scuff of boot jolted through my body and I found myself getting irritated at the guys being so noisy. This was bloody dangerous; you could walk right over someone and not see them, and even if you did, how would you know if it was one of us or one of them? It was amazing how Tande knew where he was and the speed with which he walked in those conditions. He had the senses of a cat, instinctively guiding us with total confidence.

At last he grabbed my shirt sleeve and placed me next to Buis on a mound of loose sand and grass. As my eyes adjusted to the surroundings, a double track about ten metres in front of us was vaguely visible. We lay down in a line on the mound with the MAG LMG at the top end. Jules and Smitty were busy on the other side of the track setting up a trip flare, and in a few minutes the ambush was set.

It was a long shot by any standards, but at least we were relatively safe. Pinpointing our position with mortars would be impossible in such thick bush, and in retrospect camping at the crocodile hole was about as stupid as it gets in military terms. The gooks would have had weeks to plan that attack; they could have measured out the range by foot and it was no wonder the barrage was so accurate. A 'clusterfuck' as the Americans called it.

We had to trust that Tande had made the best decision. These trackers had been known to deliberately lead patrols away from the enemy on occasions because they were scared, but most often they placed the patrol in a position of superiority, which helped a lot when the enemy's bush skills far exceeded those of a bunch of kids fresh out of high school.

This had turned into one hell of a long night and even with the adrenalin and extreme danger, I found it difficult to keep my eyes open. Time dragged on and on and I was sure some of the guys were taking naps, but it was impossible to tell. Who would believe a sandy bank full of dry grass, twigs and leaves could be so comfortable. My mind started wandering, thinking about home, my dogs, my buddies, and this chick I had been eyeballing for years. My mind just froze when she was around. I was out there making war, and I was more scared of a pretty girl than an enemy that wanted to kill me. Well almost.

As the flare went off I instinctively pulled the trigger and my R1 roared into life, blasting out a dozen rounds on auto. The rifle leaped in my hands as the bullets ripped into the bush and simultaneously the whole section followed as the bush opposite us erupted in a frenzy of smoke, debris and spitting red tracers. I saw a shadowy figure fleeing from the track so I pulled the rifle in his direction and let rip. After a few more rounds my rifle stopped and I battled furiously to change the magazine, but by the time it was loaded the flare had died down and it was all over. Some of the troops continued to fire into the dark.

"Cease fire!!" Buis barked. We were shouting and swearing in the excitement and my ears were ringing loudly again. Buis and Stander both bellowed for silence. We lay patiently for a few minutes. "Throw another flare," Buis told Jules, which he did, but there was no sign of anyone, dead or otherwise, on the track. It was unbelievable that anything could have survived that and I was more than a little disappointed that we seemed to have missed them. We talked quietly for a bit and most of us agreed there were four of them walking north and had run into the bush away from the track. There was no doubt they were taken completely by surprise, and again I was amazed at Tande's bush skills.

I switched on the radio and told Sunday about the ambush. We could not move until sunrise, so I settled down again. Buis organized a beat, but most of the guys could not sleep and were whispering excitedly in the pitch dark. I fell asleep without a problem, lying face down in the sand.

❖❖

As the sun started lighting up the horizon, the bush slowly took form in front of us. I called the base and Marais advised that Sunday had left already with alpha and bravo sections. For the first time since the stonking a few hours ago, I could see the other guys in my section, and it was almost comical how filthy we all were. The fine dust had caked itself on our sweat, and our browns were smeared with dirt and cinder ash. The whites of our eyes contrasted starkly with the rest of our bodies. I had a large patch of dried blood on my shirt from lugging Blake along the riverbank. The flies were already buzzing incessantly around us, and the whole area was littered with empty cartridges. The net effect of the barrage of rifle fire on the bush opposite us was zero, with a few flecks of tree bark missing here and there, and the two burnt flare casings lying in the sand.

On Buis' command we cautiously got up in a line and moved across the ambush area towards the *shonna*. We stopped often, crouching down and peering into the bush ahead because it was now our turn to be ambushed. Somehow I felt more composed, although still very wary, but not suffering from the paralyzing terror and indecision of last night. I was a good twenty metres away from Tande as he looked intensely at the tracks left by the fleeing gooks. Every now and then he pointed to the ground, Buis nodded his head knowingly, and I gathered there were drops of blood, indicating one of them had been hit but it didn't slow them down.

I could faintly hear the Hyena and two Bedfords in the distance grinding through the bush. I was sure Sunday would lead them along the tree line on our side of the *shonna*, and not on the tracks in case some landmines had been planted in the night. Their arrival was very comforting, and the enemy would be wise to move out quickly or face Sunday and a fresh batch of troops. I turned on the radio and gave him our position. Soon enough the three vehicles were lumbering across the flat grassland towards us.

"You blokes look like shit," Sunday looked down at us from the top of the Hyena with an amused smile as the two Bedfords pulled up behind him. "Reload your magazines and have something to eat." I had no idea that a slice of white bread and a pilchard washed down with water could taste so good.

The troops in the two Bedfords were looking at us with a mixture of shock and wonder. In the two months we had been there, this was the first time any of us had seen action, and there was fear and anticipation on their faces. We, Charlie section, were now battle-hardened soldiers, and Smitty, Freddie and Wayne were laying it on thick recounting the events of the night to the wide eyed newcomers, conveniently leaving out the panic, fear, indecision and exhaustion. Neglecting to mention the fact that if Buis had not moved us out of the camp when he did, we would all be going home "on the front page of the *Sunday Times*."

Sunday called the section leaders, trackers and signallers together for a briefing. "Blake is fine. The doctors are worried about blood poisoning at this stage and he nearly died of shock, but he is stable and will be going back to the states soon." With the pleasantries over his tone changed.

"Now, I will take Alpha section and follow the tracks while Bravo and Charlie move to this point." He pointed a meaty finger to a fork in the bush track, on a map that had seen better days. "Charlie will set up an ambush at the fork, and Bravo will sweep towards Alpha." He indicated the directions of Alpha and Bravo that would cover the most ground in the shortest time. If the enemy were in between the two sections they would be driven towards us lying in ambush at the fork.

"Have you all got fresh batteries?" he asked the signallers, looking at me directly. I nodded. "Go to channel twelve." We clicked all the radios onto the same frequency.

"Now!" he said with great emphasis. "Two Alouette's are coming at 0700." This was a huge morale boost. "Captain Strydom will be in one of them and they will sweep in front of Alpha section, so we will have to move through the bush quickly. Keep as far away from the tracks as possible without losing them," he looked at Dawie, the Alpha section leader. "Don't be scared to speak to the choppers and if the shit hits the fan, don't talk a load of crap on the radio. Keep the channel open for the captain and the pilots." We got the picture. As Alpha section got off the Bedford to take up formation, we climbed on. The idea of Charlie section setting the ambush was obviously to give us a rest.

"I want the Hyena to move over to the crocodile hole to guard the kit, but don't go into the camp because it could be booby trapped. The Bedford drivers must stay on the *shonna*. Don't go through the bush for any reason. If the gooks see you it won't make much difference, but I can't take the chance of you going over a mine." He pointed out a line on the map for them to follow. "If they are stupid enough to shoot at you on the *shonna*, don't engage them; wait for the choppers. Okay now turn your hats around." We all turned our bush hats inside out to reveal a day-glo orange patch, which the choppers would be able to see clearly from the air. This plan of Sunday's was remarkable in its simplicity, and even in my cloud of fatigue I could see it working.

We moved off and got to the fork in about half an hour. The Bedfords left and we set the ambush in the trees on the north side. The MAG LMG took up a position to our left on a low bushy mound overlooking the oncoming track, so even if they came in behind us they would be exposed. We watched as Bravo section took up formation and moved cautiously into the trees. Tande was skirting the ambush area looking for fresh tracks. He seemed satisfied the gooks had not passed yet, and looked happy with the setup.

❖❖

The flies were having a ball. They were attracted to our faces and crawled into every hole in our heads and no amount of waving could chase them away. When they got tired they rested like a speckled carpet on our backs. We smelled ripe after the night's activity and were covered in sweat, dirt and blood, feeling exhausted and hungry. Any notions of fear and loathing I had for the gooks were long gone and I don't think I could have mustered anything more than indifference if I had seen them.

We all perked up when we heard the distant whine of the Alouette's engines. Not long after, two of them appeared above the tree line, climbing steadily, and started to orbit about two kilometres away. They were to sweep the bush in front of Sunday and Alpha section. The idea was to keep the enemy's heads down while the ground troops moved through the bush following the tracks.

I was impressed with Sunday's cunning. The enemy was in big trouble, and would have to move away on either flank with extreme caution to avoid being sandwiched by Bravo, ducking from tree to tree and using every bush trick they knew. The one flank led onto the open *shonna*, so they really had only one choice and that was to move south, skirting our ambush position. This was a very long way around, but their only route to freedom. As soon as Sunday saw the tracks change direction, Bravo and the Alouettes would be redirected accordingly, so sooner or later there had to be a punch-up.

Over the radio I gleaned patchy bits of information as the operation proceeded and I could sense Sunday was getting confused and frustrated. The choppers had the best view and reported no sign of activity. As Sunday and his tracker moved ahead they reported tracks coming and going in every direction, and even some that seemed to come up behind them. Both Alpha and Bravo came across odd bits of equipment here and there, which had to be checked for clues and booby traps. Of course this took time, which was a premium asset for the gooks at this stage. Eventually the two sections came together with the Alouettes circling overhead, and I realized with total amazement that the gooks had vanished. Sunday had presumed the enemy would use common logic to survive, which apparently they did not. They were not that stupid.

If I didn't know better I'd say the pilots were getting bored. Their radio conversation hinted that Sunday had lost the plot and they only had one hour of fuel left. Re-fuelling at Sifuma would take another hour and their suggestion was to return to the air base at Mpacha, then come back when we had something definite to work with. Sunday left no doubt as to the course of action and Strydom's instructions to the pilots were clear. They decided to stay and finish the job.

Sunday's next order was very strange. After chatting to Captain Strydom over the radio for a while he directed the Alouettes over our position and then to the south. Either they had worked out the tactics the gooks were using or they were taking a huge gamble.

He then set Alpha and Bravo in a line abreast formation that was about a hundred metres wide and told them to ignore any kit they saw lying around in the bush. So they started moving south but this time with much more speed.

The choppers moved over our position and started circling away. Sunday gave us, Charlie, the order to kit up and get ready to move. It was then that I clicked what Sunday was up to. The choppers had circled over us, so the gooks knew where we were. They would think the Alouettes were sweeping in front of us and so would move behind the sweep line. This would trap the gooks between the Alouettes, Alpha and Bravo sections and us.

Buis quickly changed our position to between the forks and again we waited whilst the Alouettes circled away.

We had only been waiting about ten minutes when suddenly there was a barrage of AK47 fire from the bush a few hundred metres away and the radio chatter intensified. One chopper swung sharply to the left and the 20mm cannon hanging out the door barked rapidly. The bullets exploded like grenades when they hit the trees and ground, panicking the gooks, who were shouting at each other. Now both Alouettes were orbiting and firing into the bush, the AK's were replying with much less vigour and then I saw them, about 10 of them, running towards us through the trees at a hell of a speed. "Hold fire!" Buis shouted, but some idiot let rip, and immediately the gooks changed direction. They were now running across our line of fire and they were impossible to hit at such a distance.

"Advance line abreast!" We got up as one and started running towards them. I felt the excitement surge as the adrenaline kicked in and my heart hammered with anticipation. When they saw us some of them started shooting wildly as they ran, the bullets cracking as they passed us, but they had broken ranks and were panicking. We returned fire as one of the choppers passed overhead and as the cannon barked, one of them leapt sideways and lay there. They evaporated into the trees as quickly as they had appeared.

The Alouettes called us to stop the pursuit, and moved ahead searching the bush intensely, but they were gone. Occasionally the cannon blasted a few rounds, but the radio was quiet, so I guessed it was over for now.

When we reached the body of the dead gook, I was shocked. The damage done by the Alouettes cannon was devastating. He was literally blown to pieces, the remains of his body held together by his blood soaked fatigues.

The next surprise was a very pleasant one. Two Pumas thundered over us with fresh troops from Kwando on board, who would land ahead of the enemy to act as stopper groups while the Alouettes refuelled at Sifuma. Buis signalled for us to get ready for the Pumas and a few minutes later one of them returned and we loaded the gook's body up and clambered on board. We took off and were back at Sifuma within a few minutes.

Arriving back at Sifuma was like checking into a five-star hotel. The shower was hot for a change, compliments of Marais making the fire. We got a tin of baked beans, two slices of bread and a cola each, which tasted as good as any fillet steak or lobster I can remember. The war stories would keep us going for many weeks and I worked out we only had two more patrols before we went back to Kimberly. As long as I got my mail from home and the beers were reasonably cool it was survivable.

The ops report we got from Mpacha the next day congratulated us on a successful operation, confirming a final count of nine enemy dead and one of us wounded. There was hot discussion among us that one had got away. No mortars were found, so they might still be buried out there somewhere to this day. All our kit at the crocodile hole was recovered but we never returned there after that, all our patrols being strictly executed as we had been trained.

❖❖

Apart from Blake there were no other casualties while we were on the border, although I personally had a few close shaves. A buddy of mine dumped a loaded Bren gun in one of the mortar pits and it went off, firing a shot into the top line of sandbags. But for the sandbags the bullet would have passed through my hips. Since then I have this thing about old or obsolete firearms. Another time we were driving through the bush and this trigger-happy idiot in my section lifted his R1 and fired at a monkey in a tree behind me. He missed my head by a fraction.

When our replacements arrived a few days before we went home, they had been in the camp less than an hour when one of them blew his hand off playing with a Browning pistol; a very bad precedent in my humble opinion. When we got back to Kimberly we heard that another one of them had died after falling off the back of the infamous Bedford.

While we were in the bush all our communication was done in Afrikaans and consequently I had to speak Afrikaans in order to get by. The net result of this was that, as my Afrikaans got better, my nickname was abbreviated to "*Engelsman*". *Eventually* I became so fluent, that after a while, when I finally got back to civvy street people used to ask me what my home language was.

❖❖

The return to Kimberly marked the rundown of national service and the last three months were to be very laid back. We were soon to be "*oumanne*" with "*min dae*" (less than forty days left) and although we continued our training the intensity was a thing of the past and all the intimidating things they threw at us were now merely routine, even the pole PT. There was a bunch of us that had become good friends. We spent the evenings playing our guitars, were allowed a few beers in the mess, and only had to keep the bungalows neat and tidy.

Some bright spark decided we should have one final inspection, which we organized as a competition between the sections with Captain Strydom as the judge. We went ape again for one last time and had the place sparkling in a few hours, achieving what would have taken us a whole weekend in the past. The captain really battled to make a decision, which was a huge compliment to all of us – in a military sort of way.

At one point my section was discussing what lines of work we had planned when we hit civvy street and I was very surprised that most them, including Buis, who always seemed so organised, had nothing to look forward to. When I left school I applied for a student job with one of the mining houses which I had thought was quite a modest start, but none of them had any serious plans and no one wanted to stay in the army, although I suspect a few had secretly signed on as permanent force.

We had been back a week or so when out of the blue I was called to our captain's office. He told me, with a hint of envy, that I had been selected for pilot training. I was to report to the Air Force Gymnasium in Valhalla immediately!

4
The CO

"Merry, merry men are we
There's none so fair
As can compare
With the boys of CFS"
'Old King Cole' lyrics

We spent the first day getting our Air Force kit organised, and I felt quite strange in my fresh new blue open necked shirt and trousers, with shoes instead of boots. In our kit was a small white plastic ribbon that had to be trimmed to a regulation size and placed on our epaulettes which denoted the rank of Candidate Officer or 'CO', a very low form of life in the military that fitted in somewhere between a "*roofie*" and a lance corporal. A CO was roundly disrespected by all and sundry. We had to endure all manner of duress and provocation, but we soon discovered that being a successful CO was one of the keys to a successful career as an officer. The equivalent of a *roofie* in flying training lingo is "*pupe*" – short for pupil pilot, and these were the titles we lived with until we got our wings.

While I was getting organized, a strangely familiar voice said, "Beats being a pongo, huh?" I looked around and there was the bloke that had been sitting next to me on the rugby field when the Puma visited us in Kimberley. His name was Jim Summers. As it turned out there were two pilot selections and he had been on the second one. Jim had done his border stint at Kwando and how we had missed each other up to now was quite odd. He said he had seen me at the selection board but thought he would save both of us some embarrassment if we did not get in. It was great to have someone I knew, but that would not last for long because within a day, the whole course were buddies anyway. We had a chat and a bit of simple arithmetic showed us that there had been over seven hundred applicants, with only forty-two of us selected, so we were indeed very privileged to be there.

Our *ab initio* training was done on Harvards at Central Flying School (CFS) Dunnottar near Springs. The red brick buildings, corrugated hangars and grass runways, plus the droning of the Harvards, gave the base a Second World War atmosphere. It harked back to an era of dashing young moustachioed men whistling Glen Miller tunes and scratching in an Ouma Smuts tin for a fag, ready to take on the Hun for King and Country and to be the first choice for any mother's daughter.

Well in our case the last point could be argued at length, but we were generally a wholesome bunch. The big thing was that we had a lot in common with each other and we soon found ourselves being invited to each other's homes, enduring the scrutiny of the moms and dating the sisters. We bonded very quickly, most of the friendships existing to this day. I can only recall two incidents when things became unpleasant during our training and they both amounted to nothing. Most of the taboos I had experienced in the Army did not exist in the Air Force, like the English/Afrikaans issue and the *oumanne/roofie* thing that had led to violence at times. Even our instructors were friendly with us after hours, although an uncompromising and strict attitude existed when training.

The standards were quite high with 60% required to pass an exam and some of the tests like aircraft technical and emergencies needed 100%. If you failed two tests you got "washed". We were a few *pupes* thinner on the ground after a few weeks and we had yet to start flying. The marks were generally around 80%, but I for one had never studied harder in my life, spending an average of five hours a day buried in my books after supper and seldom getting to bed before midnight. Some of the guys were amazingly bright, just laying on their beds reading the notes like a novel and falling asleep at nine, then getting in the high nineties for the exam. Others plugged it out until three in the morning passing on sheer determination, whilst the rest simply did not make it. Luckily for the English students most of the notes were ex-Royal Air Force and consequently in English, although you could write the exams in either language. The Afrikaans guys, to their credit, did not seem to find this a problem. Another thing that could cost you dearly was making an error on your exam paper; any crossing out or adjustments, or even untidy handwriting and the whole page would be left unmarked. This was another way of teaching us not to make mistakes, a rule of thumb for flying.

Flying the Harvard was a unique experience because they had been modified very little since the Second World War. The cockpit was quite crude; the tubes of the fuselage frame and all related mechanicals exposed, the instrument panel vibrating in time with the old Pratt and Whitney radial engine. The seat was a ply and metal frame that held your parachute, strapped to your backside, firmly in place. The skin of the aeroplane itself was an aluminium and tin alloy that was apparently used to make tin cans in the old days and so earned it the nickname of "spam can" or "spammy," spam being the American version of bully beef. The primary control surfaces were covered in fabric and the control stick was made of hickory, adding to the authentic vintage appeal of the aircraft. It could also be a bit tricky to fly and was known to "bite" the unwary student "in the arse". Usually by dropping a wing or rolling to one side suddenly as a result of low speed when you were coming in to land, or excessive G forces when doing a manoeuvre. Ground loops, an uncontrolled swing when taxiing, and wheels up approaches were the kind of thing that happened to a pilot only once because they were so unpleasant. Not only were these chilling experiences, which fortunately seldom ended in catastrophe, but if you did perform a wheels up approach you were made to carry a pair of bicycle wheels around with you for a week and a ground loop was punished by making you wear your cap and tie back to front. It was a wise pupe who learned from the mistakes of others. My instructor said there were two types of pilots: 'those who have done a wheels up and those who haven't'.

As the training progressed, we became a lot more familiar with the different types of aircraft in the SAAF. One of the hangars at Dunnottar was occupied by half a dozen Pumas that were in storage for some reason and they had to be flown every now and then to check their serviceability. This also gave the instructors who were rated on them a chance to keep their hand in. They used us to practice their hoisting and took us for spins over the surrounding *mielie* fields at ultra low level. Again I was deeply impressed and had no doubt in my mind that I wanted to fly them once I got my wings. Most of us had not really decided what we wanted to fly and I had entertained ideas of flying jets on occasions, but this exposure to the Puma settled it once and for all.

Whoever chose the Puma as our medium sized chopper was a wise man. The only other chopper I can think of comparing it to in that era is the American Bell UH-1 "Huey" that has since become an icon of the Vietnam War, but the Puma was a lot more sophisticated in many respects; it had two engines, a cavernous and unobstructed interior, was faster and a heck of a lot quieter, all of which is critically important in many military operations. As sophisticated as it was, it was a tough workhorse, very reliable and could remain airborne with considerable battle damage; a gentleman's helicopter. I also noticed early on at Dunnottar that the instructors who were chopper pilots seemed to be a bit more laid-back than the others and I found it easier to identify with them.

During our stay at "Dunnos" we had a mini air show one afternoon when four brand new Mirage F1 fighters paid us a visit and did some low level aerobatics. The addition of the F1 to the SAAF fleet had not yet been officially announced by the government and still enjoyed rumour status, so it was a treat for us and very impressive. The performance by these elegant, sleek and very noisy jets stopped all the traffic on the road outside the base as they did formation and solo aerobatics. At one point, one of them flew past with its undercarriage and flaps down at low speed when the pilot inexplicably decided to do a roll. As the F1 became inverted it dropped alarmingly and headed straight for the crowd of civvies standing next to the road. He took power and lifted away with incredible agility but it scared the shit out of the motorists and, within about ten seconds, there was a traffic jam as they all struggled to get the hell out of there. We had a good laugh, but it was a very close shave.

No sooner had the Mirages left than we had a very pleasant surprise. The SAAF Museum's Spitfire "Evelyn" appeared from nowhere and gave us an unforgettable display of low level aerobatics that was every bit as impressive as the F1s. Sadly it was damaged at an air show a few years later and sold off overseas. Hence we lost another part of our precious aviation heritage. The flying was very good at Dunnos and the Harvard was a fine trainer in many respects. Not only was it a bit of a challenge to fly, but the instruments in most of the planes were so old that the needles in some of them hung or vibrated to the point where you had to compensate for the inaccurate readings. Furthermore, each plane was slightly different with its own set of quirks. This added to the skill level required to pass a test and of course the instruments in the rear cockpit, where the testing officer was seated, were again slightly different to the front. The discrepancies were not big but the limits that we had to fly within were very tight. In one respect this was good because it made us cross-reference with the other instruments to achieve accurate flying.

But there were many things that had to be checked constantly to fly this plane properly and the trap was set for the unwary pilot as soon as he started the pre-flight inspection. One careless station pilot went to Rand Airport to collect a Harvard that had just been serviced and didn't realise the aileron cables had been crossed by mistake. As any pilot knows, checking the full, free and correct movement of the ailerons is one of the pre-takeoff checks on any aircraft, but this guy thundered down the runway oblivious to the problem and found out the hard way when he lifted off. He stuck a wing tip into the runway and spun around like a scrap yard whirlwind, tearing the undercarriage and flaps off and ending up on the grass in a huge cloud of dust and gravel. Fortunately he wasn't injured, but as I explained earlier, this plane could bite you in the arse.

The first solo flight was a big issue for most *pupes*. This happened between twenty one and about twenty eight hours flying time and you had to do one circuit around the airfield on your own for the first time. I was really nervous and also the first *pupe* on the course to go solo, so I had the added pressure of everyone monitoring the pending disaster, but it went without a hitch and I landed all smiles and got hauled off by a bunch of buddies and thrown into a pond full of mud. This tradition goes way back in flying history and it marks the first waypoint in the career of any SAAF pilot. I'll never forget my instructor Mike Rennie's words as he climbed out of the Harvard before sending me off on my own. I was expecting some comforting words of encouragement, but instead I got, "OK shithead, when you kill yourself out there I'll be in the crew room knazzing a coke." But there wasn't much chance of me blowing it, because he had drilled me mercilessly from the beginning and accepted nothing less than perfection.

There are hundreds of stories about the antics of the *pupes* and the Harvard and fortunately most of them end in tears and not disaster, which is a credit to both the aircraft and the standard of training. I will share two such stories that I thought were quite amusing.

Part of our training involved low flying which is a real rush if you are not used to it. The dynamics of flying the plane low level are quite different to flying at altitude along with the very real danger of obstacles such as power lines, high ground and the complications of varying wind patterns. We were not allowed to do low flying without an instructor in the aircraft, but if we were practicing a forced landing while flying solo we ended up very close to the ground; the temptation to extend the overshoot by a mile or two and so do a bit of low flying, was hard to resist. One day a *pupe* landed after a solo period and found his instructor and the base commanding officer waiting for him. He had been reported flying dangerously low by one of the local farmers, which he denied vigorously. However, on inspecting the Harvard they found the remains of a chicken stuck in the engine cowling that the *pupe* had hit during his escapade.

The other story involves a cross-country flight for navigation training. The *pupe* was lost and was scanning the countryside around the aircraft for clues, trying desperately to match the features on the ground to the map in his hand. The instructor smelled a fish and decided to have a bit of fun with him.

"Where's Elandra?" the instructor asked the *pupe*.

"I'm not sure lieutenant," was the reply, but it was a trick question because Elandra was directly beneath them, and the *pupe* couldn't see it because the wings of the aircraft were in the way.

The instructor suddenly rolled the Harvard upside down. "Can you see it now?" he asked sarcastically.

"Yes, lieutenant," was the sheepish reply. They flew on for a while without any problems and the instructor decided to relax. He undid his harnesses and put his feet up on the exposed framework underneath the instrument panel and sat there sipping a coke.

As they were flying over Delmas, the instructor decided to check on the pupes progress. "Where's Delmas?" he demanded.

The *pupe* did not hesitate and flipped the Harvard inverted and said with great authority, "There it is lieutenant!" Meantime the instructor had fallen out of his seat and was trapped upside down on the canopy with coke pouring all over him.

By the time our training at Dunnottar was over there were thirty of us left. Most of the guys that got washed had failed exams or flying tests. One left because he didn't like the disciplined life and another broke a leg playing rugby. During our time there we only had one chap forced land due to carburettor icing and a few did wheels up approaches, but all in all we came away unscathed and were ready for Langebaanweg and the Impala jet.

Our departure from Dunnottar was marked by our first formal dinner, which ended in a butter fight and a dance where we invited our girlfriends to the base. Although the base was quite low tech, old and modestly equipped compared to the other bases in the SAAF, getting posted there was always a favourite with the pilots.

❖❖

Langebaanweg was a different cup of tea altogether. The whole base was a lot more disciplined and procedure driven. The buildings were brick with light blue glass surrounded by manicured lawns and tall blue gum trees that were used as wind breaks. The atmosphere was very formal and the misdemeanours that were tolerated at Dunnottar were a one-way ticket to civvy street at Langebaanweg.

Flying the Impala involved a whole new level of operations. The flight envelopes were expanded about three times compared to the Harvard and it took a few hours flying just to get used to the increase in speed alone. With this in mind it is obvious that you could get into trouble with this aircraft three times as quickly and, unlike the Harvard, which would bite you to wake you up, the Impala was unforgiving. The dangers were not immediately apparent because the plane itself was very easy to fly and, as I have said before, the standard of training was exceptional so there were no incidents on our course. The Imp was fitted with a state of the art Martin Baker ejection seat that saved many lives over the years. The instructors had a saying that summed the speed up pretty well: "If I say eject, and you say 'what,' you will be talking to yourself."

I don't remember the Impala with any particular fondness but there is no doubt it was a fine trainer. Flying low level was really exciting because you were skimming over the trees at 550 km per hour and navigating off a hand held map. If you looked down at the map for a split second there was always a chance you had flown over the road or river you were looking for and you were lost. Finding your position again could be very difficult. The secret was anticipation, or staying ahead of the aircraft and it all came together with training, time and practice.

The closest I came to writing myself off in an Imp was on a low-level navigation exercise. I remember flying down a valley looking for a farmhouse that was a turning point on my route. The other guys who had done the exercise before me said they pulled the nose up vertically when they got to the farmhouse and flew inverted over the crest of the mountain at the end of the valley. I did this and found myself upside down at about a hundred feet above the ground with 150 knots on the air speed indicator. I had no options and was fresh out of ideas. If I rolled upright I would stall, if I stayed like that I would stall and if I ejected, I would blast myself into the ground. So I just kept it inverted until I got over the other side of the mountain, with the Imp buffeting gently on the stall and me praying for a miracle. I could not believe how quickly I had got into trouble and treated the Imp with the utmost respect after that. And later, while enjoying some wide-eyed introspection on this incident over a beer, I decided that if I was going to be a chopper pilot I would not need to fly an aircraft upside down anyway.

But what made Langebaanweg special was its location. The weekends were spent in and around Cape Town and the Langebaan Lagoon and Vredenburg further to the north. I remember a *braai* we had at Paternoster, a small fishing village near Vredenburg, where we boiled a big *pootjie* full of sea water and tossed the live crayfish into it as we caught them. We sat huddled on the rocks around the fire under a dark, moody Atlantic sky with an icy wind blowing off the sea, sipping Old Brown Sherry and eating seafood fit for a king with our fingers. We also bought fresh snoek from the fishermen at Saldanha Bay for one rand a fish and *braaied* them in foil. I have yet to find a restaurant that can match the flavour of the fish that we cooked, hunched up like cavemen in the freezing cold.

Our flying training culminated with our wings parade that was held on a sunny November afternoon. This was a full military parade with a band and a company of soldiers with all the moms, dads and girlfriends flown in by Hercules. Out of the original forty two who started, twenty nine of us stood in front of the Chief of the Air Force, Lieutenant General Bob Rogers, marching up one at a time to have our wings pinned on our chests. Everyone was glowing with pride and finally we were set for our careers in aviation. Many became airline pilots after eventful military careers and are now captains on Boeings and Airbuses flying for airlines all over the world.

5
The Formal Dinner

"How thin the veneer of civilization"
Rod Briggs

We spent the next few weeks on leave over Christmas and then it was back to Voortrekkerhoogte in Pretoria for our officers training course. This consisted of lectures in administrative subjects with respective exams, a little bit of PT which was a largely uneventful episode, culminating in a fitness test over ten kilometres and a four day, one hundred kilometre, hike along the Magaliesburg mountains. But by far the most memorable event at the SA Air Force College (SAAFCOL) was the formal dinner that marked the end of our course.

As I walked into the mess pub, the first thing I noticed was the noise. The room was packed with blue uniforms and everyone was trying to talk above the general volume, with the occasional bellow of laughter and the tinkling of glass coming from the bar. The haze of cigarette smoke and the smell of freshly poured beer added to an atmosphere that was more festive than formal. We were all dressed in our full blues, freshly ironed and neat as pins; on our best behaviour as one would expect at a function of this importance. The idea was to have a few beers and a chat before sherry was served, and as we had all passed our officer's course I guess we had something to celebrate.

Most of us were the pilots fresh out of flying training at Langebaanweg, and with the rank of candidate officer and our wings, we stood on the threshold of our careers armed with a lot of knowledge, very little experience and heaps of enthusiasm.

The others in the group were a mixture of admin, stores and intelligence personnel who were often quite bewildered by us lot during the training. But it did not really matter what they thought, we just stuck together like glue. Although most of us had never met before we joined the Air Force, the last fifteen months of intensive flying training had bonded us in a way that defies explanation. We had become a brotherhood that exists to this day, some thirty years later.

I got a beer and settled into a conversation with a few of my buddies that revolved around how one of us had got into trouble for inviting a very pretty lieutenant on a date. We discovered that it was not so much the invitation itself, but the manner with which the invitation was executed. In a fit of beer-fuelled fearlessness, this bloke had knocked on the door of her quarters one evening and when she didn't respond, had entered the room only to find it empty. Hearing her coming along the passage behind him and with his senses dulled to the point of stupidity, he hastened into her bathroom to hide and closed the door. A few minutes later she came into the bathroom starkers and, to her horror, discovered a drunk and very apologetic pilot inviting her out for movies and steak. Her follow up was merciless. He spent the next two weeks doing extra duty under the guidance of a gym corporal, a sobering experience by any standards and earned the scorn of every female staff member on the base.

We stood there chatting and out of the corner of my eye I noticed a group of the guys standing by the bar. It looked as if they had been drinking for a while and with even my with my limited experience of these formal functions, I judged this to be a mistake. Some of them were quite merry, laughing and joking and one of them, my good buddy Stevie, was even starting to look a bit sleepy, not a good sign at this early stage in the proceedings. I was curious to see a full bottle of brandy on the bar next to them as takeaways were not allowed, when someone mentioned that it was for the kitchen and that Stevie had forgotten to give it to the chefs.

After a while, the colonel in charge of the dinner stood up from his place at the corner of the bar, traditionally reserved for the Officer Commanding, and made his way to the sherry table. We finished our drinks and followed him through to the entrance of the mess hall where a linen covered table stood with a large bronze statuette of the Air Force eagle at its centre, surrounded by dozens of sherry glasses, all of which were filled to the brim. The procedure and indeed the polite thing to do, was to sip the sherry slowly to prepare one's palate for the meal. But Stevie and the group of guys in party mode had guzzled back quite a few by the time the dinner bell tinkled. Shortly therafter, I noticed an irate chef walk smartly out of the kitchen and take the bottle of brandy away from Stevie who was clearly not bothered that he had inconvenienced the kitchen staff.

We filed slowly into the mess hall which was a very large old room with a distinctly colonial flavour, as big as a gymnasium and with a cavernous pressed metal ceiling from which hung two dusty chandeliers and rows of swirling fans.

All the sliding windows were wide open, but this and the fans did little to ease the stifling summer heat, that was compounded by our uniforms, and we were not permitted to remove our jackets which made matters rather uncomfortable. Painted completely in white and furnished with standard military issue tables and chairs, the room was very pleasant but somehow lacked the grandeur fitting an institution of this calibre. But it had aged gracefully and absolutely creaked with tradition.

The formal dinner is actually a military parade used to mark an occasion, usually the end of a course, in which a strict set of procedures has to be followed. The entire evening is under the control of one person, the commanding officer in this case. You have to attend and will not be excused except by a doctor's certificate. Everything is done in a sequence from the way you use your cutlery to the order of the meals and the way the drinks are served. The dinner has its fair measure of theatrical pomp and circumstance as is associated with any parade and there is a rigid protocol written down in a manual somewhere. All of which is backed up by a whole string of punishments should someone be foolish enough to err from the convention. For instance, once you are seated you may not leave the table for any reason and no smoking is allowed, unless of course the commanding officer deems otherwise. The waiters are normally junior chefs smartly dressed in snow-white suits with gold buttons, trained to serve the meals and pour the wine with speed and skill. Considering every serving had to be in place before you could start eating, they were under a fair amount of pressure as they had their own set of rigid procedures to follow.

The table was set in a large "U" shape with the Officer Commanding, senior officers and dignitaries seated at the base, and the remaining members seated along the two arms on the outside, with the centre area used by the waiters for easy access to the patrons. At the head of the table this evening we had the commanding officer of the Air Force College, flanked by the Dominee on one side, who was a skinny, bespeckled and very serious young man with an air of tragedy about him. As it turned out, he was dating (no, courting is the correct term) the pretty lieutenant I mentioned earlier. Having such a serious boyfriend might partially explain her severe attitude to wayward pilots. On the other side was our guest of honour, a very portly, bearded ex-Royal Navy officer with a huge red nose who was an eminent expert on pyrotechnics. Our training officers, all of whom we knew very well at this stage, made up the rest.

I positioned myself next to the guys that had been drinking, as I felt this had the most potential for entertainment in what could turn out to be a long sitting. The room hushed and we stood for grace. Then the Dominee unwittingly made his first blunder of the evening. He let forth a mournful lamentation on gratitude, moderation, and self discipline that was totally out of key with our mischievous mood, so instead of nurturing a meditation of pious introspection in each of us, he was actually fuelling the communal evil that we pilots were so well known for.

We sat down and I noticed the commanding officer was already eyeing Stevie with suspicion, as he was beginning to slouch in his chair with a big grin on his dial. Meanwhile his drinking partners, Mike and Andy, were giving the waiter a hard time about the melon sorbet, insisting it should be served at the end of the meal. Stevie started spreading the sorbet onto a roll and putting the mint leaf aside, announcing that he would smoke it later. The party was certainly on.

A hors-d'oeuvre of delicately shaved Parma ham and cheese with olive oil was placed in front of us. The white wine was an old Air Force favourite, a riesling chilled to one degree above freezing. The generous waiters wasted no time and I soon found myself with a second glass as the table was cleared for the main course and, in what turned out to be questionable wisdom, they left the half empty bottles of white wine behind.

The next course was roast chicken and thinly sliced beef, cooked rare and served with vegetables covered with gravy. It was mouth-watering. The red wine glasses were filled while we waited patiently for the commanding officer to start and I noticed Stevie and the boys had polished off their white wine; they were already taking long pulls on the red.

By now my alarm bells were ringing. I had drunk two beers, a sherry and a glass of white, had a full white and fresh red in front of me and would no doubt have another red during the meal. I decided to cool it, but the boys to my left were throwing the stuff down their necks at an alarming rate.

It was then that possibly the biggest problem with these dinners manifested itself. After the plates from the main course were cleared, I noticed the bloke next to me, Mike, was squirming uncomfortably in his seat. I asked what was wrong and he explained in a slurred whisper that he needed a pee, not at all surprising considering he had drunk enough to fill a dam. Now, as the reader knows, we were not allowed to leave the table at all and we had dessert, cheese and biscuits, the toasts and speeches still to go, so at least another twenty minutes. Mike was getting very uncomfortable so I suggested he slash in an empty wine bottle, which he found very funny. The idea must have floated around in his brain for a while. Slowly it turned from outrageous to quite sensible until, without warning, he reached over to the white wine bottle in front of us, poured the remains into his glass and placed the bottle between his legs. The expression on his face changed from desperation to peaceful relief and then in a barbaric act I did not anticipate, he placed the wine bottle back on the table. The waiters, who were clearing the tables in efficient silence, respectfully left the half full bottle where it was.

Apart from this, the evening was going extremely well. The food was way above average for Air Force fare, the cooks and waiters had not missed a beat and the commanding officer and our guest were chatting away merrily; our guest clearly comfortable in these formal surroundings, washing down his meal with vast quantities of wine. So far the dignity of the occasion had been further elevated by our good behaviour, and even Stevie and the boys had managed to hold their pose admirably.

A dessert of ice cream and brandy cake was served next, which had to be accompanied by a small traditional ceremony whereby the commanding officer would light his serving. He offered the privilege to our guest, who accepted, as we all glowed with sentimental warmth. Then the head waiter strutted out of the kitchen with the bottle of brandy Stevie had earlier, balanced delicately on a silver tray. He removed the cap and poured it over the cake with a flourish, produced a box of matches and with great ceremony struck a match, holding it to the cake. The match burned with all of us looking on expectantly, but nothing happened, to the point where it started to burn his fingers and he tossed it onto the tray. He tried again with no luck.

Stevie, Mike and Andy were giggling all the time this was going on and I asked Mike what the joke was. He whispered that they had drunk some of the brandy before the meal and topped the bottle up with water, thus explaining why it would not burn. By now the commanding officer, the guest and the waiter were all striking matches and holding them to the cake, to no avail. I had to give them full marks for determination as this carried on for a few minutes and eventually all three of them, plus a few of our training officers were hunched over the cake, feverishly fiddling with boxes of matches and cigarette lighters, when suddenly the brandy ignited with an impressive whoosh and all of them sprung back in surprise. Our guest had a problem though; his beard was aflame and he started beating at it furiously with a meaty pair of hands as smoke and sparks billowed out of the confusion. The commanding officer panicked at the sight of this and reached for the only extinguisher he could find, a half-full bottle of red wine and showered it over his head.

Eventually things settled down and after profuse apologies all round they sat down and nibbled nervously at the cake, which commanded great respect at that stage.

Of course, the hilarity of this disaster was not lost on the three rogues next to me who were congratulating each other heartily.

Our guest was in a sorry state as he had lost the left side of his beard, his left eyebrow, and a handful of hair from the side of his head. This had the odd effect of giving his face two distinctly different expressions. On the right he was scowling with disapproval, and on the left he looked pleasantly surprised, with the two expressions divided by a big red nose. What was left of the poor man's frazzled beard stood at right angles to his very pink cheek and he now looked like an experimental pyrotechnic walrus, that had been dressed up as a penguin and used to bait a killer whale. I wondered how he would explain this one to his mates at the Royal Navy club.

The three characters who had engineered this event had finally drunk all the wine and had only the port to look forward to, which would be served with the cheese and biscuits during the speeches. Stevie was now quite pickled and I noticed him staring blankly at the floor in front of us with his head cocked at an odd angle. For a moment I thought he was contemplating the last bottle still on the table, but then realized he was looking across the room at Jim who was crawling on his hands and knees behind the other table. Jim, always a willing contributor to any kind of mayhem, had made his way to the floor in front of the commanding officer under the main table. Because of the size of the table he was hidden from the dignitaries and of course we all pretended not to notice. He very delicately tied the Dominee's shoe laces together, eyed our guest's laces for a while but no doubt thought he had had enough for one night and then crawled carefully back to his seat.

This had diverted my attention away from my buddies next to me and when I looked again, Stevie still had the blank stare on his face, but the blurred focus had shifted to the dreaded wine bottle full of pee on the table that everyone had avoided so carefully. He was clearly amazed at finding so much wine on the table so late in the meal. Mike, of course, was sitting dead still, holding his breath and waiting for disaster to strike for the second time this evening. I tried to warn Stevie but with a surprisingly deft hand he reached over and filled his glass and then took a long pull. He sat bolt upright with his eyes bulging, and in a desperate effort to control himself dribbled the ghastly fluid all over the front of his immaculate full blues. He then stood up, took three flat-footed steps backwards and leapt head first through the open window behind us and crashed into the shrubs below, retching wickedly. This was so funny the guys on our side of the table needed a few minutes to stop laughing, but no one else in the room seemed to notice what had happened and they were all looking at us wondering what the fuss was about.

At this stage the cheese and biscuits arrived with the port, and the commanding officer allowed us to smoke while we listened to our guest speak on the dangers of fireworks and some of his experiences in the Royal Navy. This went on for far too long and we were getting very restless by the time he had finished. The commanding officer then gave a short speech and thanked our guest. Finally, we all stood for a toast to the State President, at which point the Dominee teetered unsteadily for a few seconds as he tried to figure out what was wrong with his feet and then plunged sideways, grabbing wildly at the commanding officer and the table. The commanding officer saw what was coming and took a quick step backwards to get out of the way. Meanwhile the Dominee headed for the floor, taking the tablecloth and contents of the table with him, accompanied by an almighty crash of cutlery. The entire table of dignitaries and a whole herd of waiters rushed out of the kitchen to help him. They managed to sort the mess out in quick time and he escaped with no more than a red face and a few smears of butter on his dinner jacket. The commanding officer, however, had a sense of humour failure. The combination of events was a little too contrived for his liking and he was searching for the culprits. He had pilots leaping out of windows, shoe laces tied together and an inexplicable fire that had to be accounted for. In a tense statement he advised us these matters would be taken up in the morning, but he should have known better than to try and use fear as a weapon because we just laughed him off.

We all stood in respectful silence while the commanding officer and dignitaries left the room in single file. The reader should not be mistaken by thinking that the events of the evening were over because, as I have tried to illustrate, we were capable of much more abominable behaviour.

The last of the head table had no sooner left than the first curl of butter sailed across the room and splattered on the wall behind me, missing a picture of one of our past Prime Ministers by a whisker. A war of butter and bread roll slinging erupted in an instant, with the admin girls squealing as they fled to preserve their uniforms and their hair. I ducked out quickly in a vain effort to preserve my own uniform, and headed for the mess pub.

The next morning was spent cleaning up the disaster area. The commanding officer had obviously endured many of these formal dinners over the years as he had cheered up considerably and took it very much in his stride, so nothing too serious came of it.

Many times during the course we got into trouble and more often, than not, the punishment just strengthened our bond, with no ill feelings against the perpetrators.

Yep folks, these are the guys that use the phrase, "Good day ladies and gentlemen, this is your captain speaking".

6

Chopper Training

To fly is heaven, to hover is divine.

At the end of our SAAFCOL training the pilots had a sort of mini selection board with a group of our instructors. We filled in a small form that asked us what was our first and second choice for the aircraft we wanted to fly. Jim and I put our heads together and decided to put down choppers only, with no second choice. What you asked for and what you got depended on your marks during the wings training and we had both done quite well, especially Jim, who had surprised everyone because he was so full of crap but also very bright. So we felt that we should state our case for choppers very clearly. My interview only lasted about thirty seconds so I was quite sure I was on my way to Bloemfontein. We had also been together since basics in the Army and had got everything we asked for from the Defence Force so far, so I guess there was a bit of ra-ra-ree between the two of us as well.

We spent Easter at our homes and then I drove down to Durban for a week with Jim's family at their invitation. While down there I met one of Jim's friends, Vanessa, and we spent a lot of time together during the week. We got on really well and this was one of the things that made me decide to apply for a posting in Durban when I finally qualified on Pumas. Jim was absolutely hell bent on getting posted to Durban and the climate was also more pleasant than JoBurg.

Jim's old folks were also taking a shine to me, and I really enjoyed their company as well. They were so down to earth and in all the time I had spent with them, I had never heard any of them cross words.

❖❖

We arrived at AFS Bloemspruit in mid January, and settled into our bungalows with Jim and I sharing a room. Lectures, mainly helicopter aerodynamics, commenced and soon we were preparing for our first flight in the Alouette III.

It really is amazing that a chopper actually flies. The complexity of the rotors and equally as complicated aerodynamics, inherent instability and extremely high maintenance and running costs place it in the miracle category.

The "Alo", however, was as competent as it was quirky. On the way out to the training area on my first flight I had a strange feeling that we were flying slightly sideways. In fact we were, as the turn and slip indicator showed and then the instructor pointed out a piece of string, on the canopy outside the cockpit that showed, according to the air flow, that we were flying straight! This was due to the position of the tail rotor, all explained in detail in our lectures. This became worse in the hover and after half an hour of flapping around an area the size of a rugby field and using every trick of co-ordination I had ever learned, I decided the Alouette was impossible to fly.

When we got back, I was relieved to discover that all my buddies had had a similar experience. Over the next few days things improved slightly, then suddenly I clicked and the Alouette became an absolute joy to fly. The secret was not to fly it, but to "think" it, to let it become an extension of your body and mind.

Bloemfontein, in my humble opinion, was not the most exciting place in the world. Being so small and stuck in the heart of the maize belt it was a very conservative city and being an outsider didn't help at all. The locals treated us with detached suspicion and unless you were married, there was no social life and little chance of getting a girlfriend. Jiggs, as he had become known to us because he was always hungry, and I decided it was time to brush up on our golf. He had played for his school and had no problem getting back to a five handicap and I ploughed a respectable twenty four, under his watchful guidance. Being Defence Force members it cost us peanuts to play at the local club, so we grabbed every opportunity to squeeze in a round. I also learned to play bridge and a number of other card games. These would stand me in good stead for the rest of my SAAF career, because once the lectures were finished we had quite a bit of spare time between the flying.

Training on the Alouette was a great experience and I have yet to find a chopper pilot who flew them that doesn't have the greatest respect for them.

The acid test came when we did our night flying training. We went deep into the GF and set up a few torches on a riverbank to act as markers for our landings. It was pitch dark, and the human eye changes substantially with darkness so it was very difficult, if not impossible, to judge height and distance. The whole exercise came down to procedures where all the turning points were pre-determined and speed and rate of descent had to be strictly controlled. We did a few landings and then the instructor, Neall, told me not to use the landing light anymore, so we took off into the darkness and did a circuit using the very basic instruments of the aircraft. The air was dead still so every tiny movement of the collective and cyclic seemed to be amplified and Neall pointed this out, asking me to fly as smoothly as possible. Every movement he could feel would cost me a beer. After three circuits I got it right, and it proved that the Alouette, if set up properly could be as smooth as ice. He was satisfied and told me later that flying like that, and another manoeuvre called a short field landing, separated the men from the boys. If he was happy, I was happy, but the best was yet to come.

7
Vulture's Retreat

"Hark! hark! the lark at heaven's gate sings"
William Shakespeare

Towards the end of our operational training on choppers we spent a week in the Drakensberg Mountains for mountain flying. This is a critically important phase because, although we were reasonably proficient pilots at that stage, we still had a lot to learn in terms of experience. The effects of up-draughts and down-draughts, varying wind speeds, slope landings, rapidly changing weather conditions, hovering next to cliff faces, pinnacle landings, and of course operating at high altitude. High altitude has a phenomenal effect on a chopper because they are normally designed to operate where the air is dense, such as close to sea level. As the air gets thinner with altitude, the engines and rotor blades become less effective and the whole exercise becomes a lot more marginal. Conversely, a fixed wing aircraft is designed to be more efficient at altitude, where speed and fuel efficiency is important, whereas a chopper is designed for lifting weight and manoeuvring in confined spaces. Whatever the analogy when comparing the two aircraft types, there is one fundamental difference; they don't have nearly as much fun as we do. And what makes it even more interesting is, as we all know, man was not meant to fly and flying a chopper is one of humankinds more blatant affronts to the laws of nature.

The mountain flying course started when all of the instructors and students took off from Bloemspruit in about a dozen Alouettes and headed for James Sclanders' farm at the base of the small berg near Winterton. We had to fly around the southern side of Lesotho, which is a fair trek in an Alouette, and landed just before sunset in a large horse paddock adjacent to the farm buildings.

The immediate priority was to shower and change for an evening in the pub with the locals. Or so we thought. After the sun set the temperature dropped suddenly and by supper it was freezing cold. Just to make sure we knew who was in charge, Mother Nature sent a wind howling down from the top of the berg that threatened to turn us all into blocks of ice, so retiring early was the favoured option. This was pretty much the pattern for the duration of the course, so going out to a pub somewhere had to be planned and motivated, added to which was the question of road transport.

The day started with an early breakfast and a stroll down to the paddock at sunrise to help the engineers prepare the aircraft for the day's flying, which after a night in the open were covered in frost and surrounded by clouds of silver mist. I just remember that there were lots of grease nipples all over the moving parts of the chopper that needed to be serviced. Things have changed a lot since then. Choppers these days have maintenance-free high tech materials in place of bearings and couplings that are simply and easily replaced at regular time intervals.

The day was divided into two periods with the morning session spent under the control of my instructor Neall and in the afternoon, I went solo to practice what he had taught me. There was a lot to learn. Firstly, you had to learn how to read the wind which, to state the obvious, you cannot see, so you look at the pattern the wind is making on the grass and feel the very subtle way the chopper responds to the turbulence. We were lectured in detail on how wind flows over every imaginable object and drilled on the inherent dangers. But this had little relevance compared to the real thing. Doing a slope landing with the wind coming from the side sounds simple enough, but it is an amazingly complicated manoeuvre and goes back to my conviction, that you have to fly a chopper by the seat of your pants. If you think of how many penalty or conversion kicks rugby players miss due to the wind changing inside a stadium, then this will give you some idea of the complications.

Altitude depletes the performance and this leads me to the first part of my story. One of the lessons involved high altitude landings so we headed out over the small berg to the amphitheatre, a massive natural curved cliff face about five thousand feet high and seven kilometres long, carved out of the Drakensberg Range by God's own ice cream scoop. The top of the berg here is about ten thousand feet above sea level and the whole area is untouched by man, a quality I have come to treasure in this day and age.

The flight up took a while and the Alouette became quite asthmatic above eight thousand feet, so a long orbit was required before I saw the top of the mountains come into view. And what a glorious sight it was. The air was crystal clear and smooth as frozen silk and the view over the small berg and Natal was truly awe-inspiring. Being winter there was a fair amount of haze over the lowlands, but I have it on good authority that on a clear day you can see the sea from up there, some two hundred kilometres away. The other side of the mountains was quite flat and very rocky to the point where no man-made vehicle could pass there. Large patches of snow and ice contrasted starkly with the black volcanic rock and the only vegetation was clumps of grass scattered randomly around.

I noticed our air speed was only sixty knots and the power setting was well above cruise, so we were running out of power and the Alouette felt sluggish on the controls. The key was to fly as smoothly as possible and avoid any large or sudden control inputs, making all the angles of bank very shallow.

Neall showed me how to do a landing and then it was my turn. I had learned to be very careful with all things flying, but Neall made everything seem so easy that I was often led into a false sense of confidence, and it often surprised me how far short of his requirements I fell. And then as soon as I got the hang of it, he moved the parameters and I felt as if I was starting again. This was a perfect example.

We flew around for a while looking for a suitable landing spot which needed to be slightly raised above the surrounding area, flat and free of obstructions like boulders and sheets of ice. I found one and started the planning phase of the landing. We were quite close to the escarpment so I did an orbit over the void, because there was no wind, and battled the whole way round to maintain my altitude. I kept losing my visual references so I turned in too early and noted on my inspection run, that the landing spot disappeared underneath us because my speed was way too high and there was no way I could have landed there from that approach. Then our engineer pointed out the high gearbox oil temperature caused by the continuously high power setting and the thin air, so I had trashed my first attempt. This time I turned over the flat rocky mountain-top and picked my references with more care, extending my downwind leg by a good kilometre to give myself plenty of room. I turned onto approach for landing and gently eased the nose up to bleed off my speed. It soon became obvious that we were flying on the absolute limits of the chopper. I had almost full power on the collective and if I pulled the nose up a fraction more we lost height, so we floated on and on with the landing spot getting closer and the gearbox temp close to limits, there was no way I was going to stop in time. To my dismay the landing spot passed beneath us and I went into my third orbit. I was relieved to see the temperature falling as I extended my downwind leg for double the distance this time. Neall suggested a slightly steeper approach and the whole thing started to come together. After a heck of a long approach, where we floated on and on for ages, I touched down on the spot without too much fuss, feeling very chuffed.

A few days later we were flying around the amphitheatre again when Neall asked me if I wanted to visit Vulture's Retreat. My first thought was that this was a pub in the area, which did not make sense under the circumstances, so I said yes knowing he would not waste time on a triviality.

We flew towards the southern side of the amphitheatre and headed for the cliff face about half way up. As we got closer I imagined viewing a bunch of vultures' nests, which were very common around there, from the privileged platform of our Alouette. As we got closer, Neall did an orbit to gain a bit of height and then did a direct approach towards the sheer vertical fall of granite. We ended up in the hover about fifty feet away from the face and I still could not figure out what he was up to, when I noticed a shadow that reached almost the entire height of the amphitheatre. There were plenty of shadows so this did not mean much at that stage, but Neall was edging slowly towards this one with intense concentration. As we got dangerously close I realised that it was not only a shadow but a crack about sixty feet wide that went deep into the mountainside. But I still could not figure out what he wanted to do and I was getting a bit nervous. He edged closer and it occurred to me that he was going to do something crazy, but as I trusted him implicitly, I kept my mouth shut. But this was not crazy, it was lunacy; he was going to fly into the crack! My instincts told me that the crack was much too narrow for the Alouette and we were so close now I was waiting for the rotor tips to touch the cliff face, which would have been the end of us. But we moved slowly on, hovering forward inch by inch until the shadow enveloped the chopper and I could see into the crack. We had on each side of us two sheer cliff faces of ragged black granite, and we were inside the crack still moving carefully forward until finally the two sides came together in front of us and we could only go back. To our right there was a fairly large flat ledge and Neall moved slowly over to it and gently touched down. This was one of the most amazing and beautiful sights I have ever seen. In front of us was a frozen waterfall glistening like frosted glass that cascaded down from the mountain top thousands of feet above us and landed on the ledge where it spread into an ice sheet before it vanished over the edge and disappeared into the bowls of the mountain, thousands of feet below. It took me a while to absorb the majestic glory of this experience.

I then wondered why the Alouette was not sliding around on the ice sheet, but of course Neall was still flying it. Although we had landed, the aerodynamic forces were keeping us steady, so technically the chopper was still flying. We took off and reversed out of the crack with equal care and headed back to the farm.

We students were forbidden to enter Vulture's Retreat on our own, but Neall took me back for visit a few days later and I managed to get some snaps, but they did little justice to the place. To this day that rates as one of my most memorable flying experiences.

As with all courses we had to have a party to celebrate its successful conclusion, so a *braai* was arranged for the last Sunday we were in Winterton. This took an unusual form for us as a games day was arranged and a whole lot of the local families, from the surrounding farming community, were invited to join us. I say unusual because the standard format was to stand around drinking beer, chewing the cud and unless the wives and girlfriends were there to help us, the *braai* faded into insignificance and either did not happen or the meat was charred beyond human consumption, or both.

Everything started extremely well and, as chopper crews are generally a gregarious bunch, we got on well with our guests and had a lot of fun, with the usual clowns providing the entertainment. We had a great meal and after lunch, when most of the guests had left, we sat around the fire with a few of the locals having a chat. The conversation centred mainly around flying and life on the farms, finally ending up on the subject of hunting and the eternal debate of the best rifle calibre. I knew very little about this, but it was interesting to hear the stories placing one calibre better than the other, ranging from impressive to utterly fantastic, as the beer and brandy fuelled the story tellers' imaginations.

To prove a point, Kukes, one of our instructors, told us about his 308 and some of the animals he had hunted, swearing by its pinpoint accuracy and deadliness. The 308 was the civilian version of the old NATO 7.62 calibre cartridge that was used by the SADF for many years and a very popular calibre because you could swipe premium quality ammo from the Army and go hunting! Good thinking if your wife insists feeding the kids is more important than buying ammo.

We had been out on a bicycle race that involved a collection of bikes borrowed from the local shop owners. Floppy, one of the students on the course who was becoming quite a character in the SAAF, due to a number of infamous deeds and an outrageous sense of humour, had won the race thanks largely to a truck that had towed him most of the way. He claimed his prize, a case of beer that he handed out to everyone as a warm up to some serious drinking. Kukes disappeared for a while and returned with the rifle under discussion and I must say, it was a very impressive bit of gear. To date I had only been exposed to functional military ordnance. The rifle was passed around for a detailed inspection by everyone and I was surprised at how light it was and how comfortable it sat in my hands and shoulder. The deep blue metal was complimented by the sculptured wooden stock, whilst the telescopic sight finished the weapon off to produce an instrument of mysterious beauty.

Eventually a packet of bullets was produced and Floppy strode off a short distance, about twenty or thirty metres, placing his beer on top of his head and challenging Kukes to make good his claims of the rifles accuracy. Kukes loaded the rifle and took aim, as we all looked on in silence, but the beer kept sliding off of Floppy's head so he held it out at arms length with his fingertips. The rifle erupted with a magnificent roar and the beer can disappeared along with the end of Floppy's thumb. He crumpled up in pain, with blood squirting all over his clothes, as we all rushed forward to help him. Some of us thought he had been shot fair and square. Kukes was distraught, but when we got to Floppy he was laughing and swearing, although clearly in excruciating pain. How nobody had grasped the lunacy of this event escapes me to this day.

Now we had a problem. The nearest hospital was in Ladysmith, which was miles away. Going by road would take ages but going by chopper was impossible because we had all been drinking. While we worked this out the local doctor arrived and attended to Floppy. Then we remembered Ben, one of our instructors, had gone to church and had been invited to coffee and biscuits afterwards. There was a chance he was stone sober and one of the locals sped off in his *bakkie* to find him. We were lucky and soon an Alouette arrived from the farm and Floppy was on his way to the hospital in Ladysmith.

Stories like Floppy's thumb become legends in the SAAF. He used to score drinks in the pub by dipping the blunt end of his thumb in our beers – just didn't taste the same after that. I met a business associate recently who knew Floppy vaguely, but remembered him especially because of his thumb.

8
Puma Conversion

"A man's dreams are an index to his greatness"
Zadok Rabinowitz

Our chopper training ended in Bloemfontein with a formal dinner, which was low key for a change, not because the wives and girlfriends of the officers were invited, but because it was so cold. We decided to have a farewell *braai* as well the next day and the ice was still hanging from the overflow pipes at mid-day. The *braai* was memorable with the mess supplying delicious Karoo lamb chops and the home made *boerewors.*

Next call was Swartkops, my old stomping ground and it was good to get back to Pretoria. Bloem was just a little bit too quiet, but that said, my handicap was down to eighteen and I could hold my own in a game of Bridge, plus of course I could fly one of the best helicopters ever built. This was also my first exposure to squadron life, which was a bit like being at university for a few years and then arriving for the first day at the office. It was great; totally relaxed and I really enjoyed meeting all the characters we had heard so much about over the years.

Jim and I were together again and now we both had Durban firmly in our sights. There were only five of us on this course and we spent the first week doing the technical and emergencies in preparation for the flying phase. Then one morning I walked onto the hardstand with my instructor, Major Monster Wilkins, and stood face to face with my dream aircraft. Very impressive it was too. It was big, powerful and quite good-looking in a very functional sort of way. I realized that one of my greatest dreams had come true. Flying it was a joy, with the controls light and responsive, all power assisted and gyro stabilized. But it was a completely different animal to the Alouette III. Its weight and inertia meant you had to be thinking ahead of the aircraft, planning any manoeuvres with a thoughtful anticipation. It was also a lot faster. The first few tries I had at doing a spot landing I overshot hopelessly, whereas had I been in an Alouette, I could have plonked it down anywhere with a few flicks of the cyclic. The power delivery was also a lot slower because of its free turbine system, again requiring anticipation and you could have a very hard and untidy landing if you got it wrong.

The course included instrument flying, which was interesting in a chopper, otherwise the systems were all pretty much the same as the Alouette. Apart from having my little Mazda smashed up in a hailstorm, the course went without a hitch.

Towards the end, we did a long navigation exercise that entailed routing to Bloemfontein, Leeuwdoring in the middle of the Karoo and then an overnight in Cape Town. The next day we had to fly coastwise to Port Elizabeth and then back to Swartkops via a refuelling stop in Bloemfontein.

When we arrived at Ysterplaat in Cape Town the weather was lovely, so we hit the local restaurants to enjoy some seafood and hit the sack early. The next morning the weather was atrocious with the clouds below the tops of the surrounding mountains, patches of rain and a strong gusting wind. The other crews opted to skirt around False Bay, basically flying along the beach to P.E., but Monster pointed to our original route over the mountains at Grabouw.

"Go that way and we'll save some time. We can be first to refuel at P.E." he waved his hand nonchalantly at the clouds in front of us. His cool nerve was legendary in the SAAF and, anyway, he was the boss. I pointed the nose just north of Gordons Bay as we winged it across the Cape Flats. When we got to the mountains the cloud was patchy and I could see the ground without too much trouble, so it seemed fine to continue. However a few minutes later we were deep in the cloud so I descended a bit to keep the ground visible, but we had to go lower and lower until we were at about three hundred feet and I was only getting occasional glimpses of the ground. Now I was really starting to shit myself. Brief glimpses of Grabouw appeared below and I knew there were mountains on either side of the town. Monster looked as if he was thoroughly enjoying the ride and then he did one of the most unbelievable things I have ever seen. He put his hand into his flying jacket and pulled out a packet of sliced palony, opened it and dumped it onto the radio panel! He stuffed a few slices into his mouth and said casually, "Help yourself."

"Major, don't you think we should turn back?" I tested him. This was the most harrowing experience I had ever had in an aircraft.

"Nah bullshit, keep going, you're doing fine." He replied without a care in the world, munching away happily and so that's what I did. Sure enough the ground started to drop away and I descended out of the clouds. Soon the coast loomed through the distant mist and we were close to Gansbaai. Later Monster explained that we were in a chopper, so if in doubt, land. Now how obvious is that and about a year later, when I got "clagged in" near Ladysmith, that's exactly what I did. We enjoyed some coffee and rusks with the farmer and his wife whose paddock we had landed in and when, after half an hour the cloud had lifted, we were on our way again.

A few days later we were qualified as co-pilots, or *sandsakke,* and I received my new rank of full lieutenant, whereupon I tossed my well-worn CO stripes into the bin! The cherry on the cake was when Jim and I were told we were being posted to Durban. I then started preparing for my first operational tour: Rhodesia, soon to become Zimbabwe.

9
Mkwazine

The 'Slopies' and the 'Philistines'

The war in Rhodesia slowly eroded the resources of the white minority government until eventually it relied heavily on South Africa for support. The South Africans however had their own costly war to deal with in South West Africa/Namibia, as well as an internal armed political struggle that was gaining momentum. Gold, South Africa's most valuable export and the keystone of the economy, was losing its lustre in the eyes of the international investment community, to the point where our mines were breaking even at best and as the South African economy slowed, the Rhodesian initiative had to suffer.

In January 1980 non-partisan elections were held and although it was a foregone conclusion, that Robert Mugabe would lead the soon to be named Zimbabwe into the future, the United Nations required the South African Air Force to conduct operations in support of the elections.

The country was beautiful lush green African bush, quite flat with roughly conical hills called gommels scattered around and rivers meandering between them. From the air it could be seen how the farms were cut from the surrounding bush and the fertile soil used for tobacco and cotton crops, immaculately manicured and irrigated to an emerald green lustre.

Jiggs had been sent off to Ondangwa for his first bush tour and it was the first time we had been separated since joining the SAAF, so things felt strange. We did not live in each other's pockets but we were really good buddies and I missed his evil sense of humour.

19 Squadron shared a small base on an airfield serving a farming community called Mkwazine in the south east of the country. There was a grass airstrip that was used for crop sprayers, but it could handle an aircraft as large as a Dakota and for a short while, it was occupied by two Pumas, a number of Alouettes and a company of Army troops together with tents, vehicles, kitchen and ablution facilities; in effect, a sort of small self-contained airbase called a Tactical Airfield Unit, or TAU.

The Rhodesians, or 'Philistines' as we called them, had a very civilized approach to the war. Their officer's mess, for example, consisted of a cook and an assistant that fed the whole lot of us, about fifty people, using an old wood fired stove. The food was excellent; after all an army marches on its stomach. I even heard that if the cook made a lousy meal he could be charged! There was also very little bluster among the ranks and the whole place had an air of understated professionalism. Sometimes the British colonial insanity was unmistakable; one of their Alouette pilots used to take his dog with him on his bush tours!

Nothing much happened on this tour but there were a few incidents that made it memorable. We were on final approach to land one day when the whole camp of about two hundred soldiers ran onto the runway and gave us a "brown eye." We found this amazing sight very amusing and Mac, the guy I was flying with, swore this good natured deed would not go unanswered. I had heard of these mass brown eyes before and they were never considered insulting, but rather added to the military camaraderie between the South African and Rhodesian forces.

The Air Force quarters were at the back of one of the farmhouses on a patio that adjoined the swimming pool and *braai* area. We had our own fridge filled with beer, a record player with a few well-worn records and a rundown tennis court that was used constantly. Considering we were in a war zone these conditions were great and I have only pleasant memories of that, my first, bush tour.

One evening, when we were making our way through the farm buildings to the mess for supper, I noticed a group of Rhodesian army officers sitting on a long wooden bench, chatting over a beer and a smoke. They all turned and stared at us as we approached, and then one of them said in a sardonic tone, "Watch it, here comes the fucking Slopie Air Force."

We strolled closer and as we got next to the bloke who had made the comment, Mac suddenly pulled down his shorts, placed his arse about a foot away from his face and let off a huge fart. Then he turned around with a smile and said, "How's that for Air Force you fucking pongo?"

10
The Hot Extraction

Fame through our deeds
19 Squadron motto

After the Rhodesian tour I was only back in the states for a few days, when I had to pack for my first bush tour in South West Africa. I did not even get to Durban and my new squadron, but stayed with my folks in Johannesburg and my Dad dropped me off at Waterkloof. Without realizing it, this was an indication of the workload in store for us.

It was the end of the first week of my first bush tour at Ondangwa and I was just beginning to find my feet. This place was the centre of activity in the operational area and it could be very hectic. I had already flown about twenty five hours doing trooping and casevacs and soon found out, that you could be called at any time day or night to fulfil the duties of an aerial pack horse or sky Samaritan.

Now there is a strange phenomenon in the military that concerns disappearing kit. When you are first issued with your kit, you have to sign for it on the pretext that it will be handed back when you leave and you will have to pay for anything that is missing. I have a deeply rooted suspicion that the institution itself deliberately removes items from circulation, so that in order to preserve your own personal inventory you have to relieve others of theirs and so a kleptocratic tradition perpetuates that is as much a part of the Army as is shoe polish, plain cigarettes and coagulated oats. I have never caught a thief nor even heard of one being caught and I have certainly never been caught myself.

I was leaving the mess after breakfast one day when I heard a voice behind me. "Hey Goat, why did you join the Air Force?" Major Pine Pienaar asked sarcastically. This was a tricky one. This bloke was a jet jockey and besides not knowing him too well I was not sure of what he was getting at. Sometimes it was wise to humour your senior officers with a shallow but pleasing answer, which made me very uncomfortable as being obsequious was not my style.

"I want to fly choppers, major," I tested him politely.

"Well you got that right, but what about the rest of the job? Where is your penlight, you're wearing *veldskoene* and your bush hat is gyppoed like an ozzie hat." Why he had to piss on my battery like that was a mystery. The penlights never worked properly and wearing *veldskoene* and my hat was part of the chopper pose. "And you've got a *babbalas* (hangover)!" This point I couldn't argue. "Who the hell do you think you are man? Get your act together or I'll eat you like a *mielie*!" He turned and stalked off.

I was stung by this humiliation. My reputation was unsullied and the missing pen light had been swiped by someone who needed it urgently and would be replaced in due course. Anyway he was a jet jockey; what did he know?

Unfortunately this continued for a while and I made a habit of avoiding him in order to save myself the antagonism.

The rivalry between chopper and jet pilots or *vlamgatte* in the Air Force was legendary but never officially acknowledged and so I decided to laugh this one off. The chopper pilots had a more casual attitude to discipline and we stuck together like glue. We worked, played, fought and died together, which made for powerful bonding.

Another thing in the SAAF was giving people nicknames. By the time I had qualified on Pumas I had a number of them; Klaus, Klausie or Niklaus, Nickel-arse, Goat, Woes, Letsgo, Fuck Knuckle, Jork, Ballas … and then some. Eventually it settled on either Klaus or Ballas, and both were fine by me, with the less complimentary ones being tossed in on occasions. Jiggs got his nickname from early on in his *pupes* course because he was always looking for food. On the squadron we had Monster, Crow, Double Dave, Gees, Staal, Motomouth, Flats, Jet Jungle, Vark, Floppy, Huck, Hojan, Hobart, Dozy, Peanuts, Waterkoppie, Fink, Gringo … I could go on for ages. I wondered what the enemy thought when we spoke to each other over the radio as we all had a few names. A two Puma formation could sound like an invasion flotilla!

That morning the sun was beginning to generate heat waves off the runway from early on and the cream coloured sand and tropical palm trees shimmered in the distance. If the sea was nearby, this would have been a fabulous holiday destination, but instead it was the middle of a war zone with the local population living on the poverty line and the whole place plagued by flies and mosquitoes.

Ondangwa consisted of walls of sandbags, fifteen foot revetments made out of mounds of bulldozed sand, tin and fibre buildings covered with camo nets, heavily armed lookout towers and ack-ack installations and a massive perimeter fence. In the background was the constant drone of diesel-electric generators punctuated by jets and choppers taking off and landing. It started as a temporary airfield providing support for light aircraft and choppers, and later a large tarmac runway was built so that jets and transport aircraft could be accommodated. It had all the functions of a normal base such as a clinic, mess, stores, living quarters and ops facilities housed in tents, metal sheds or fibreboard huts. The army also had their own facilities for Parabat airborne troops and a Reconnaissance Commando company. As the war dragged on the sheds became cast concrete buildings and limited utility networks and communications were installed so that the base became a permanent and reasonably sophisticated establishment.

I made my way to the ops room dodging large puddles of rainwater from the previous night's storm, greeting people who ran the base as I went. Everyone knew everybody and there were no secrets. I pushed open the old metal door and made my way past the maps, notice boards and notices plastered all over the walls as banks of olive-green two way radios hissed and crackled in front of bored looking clerks. The air inside was uncomfortably hot and stale with the smell of smoke, cigarette butts and old coffee grinds, while the whirring fans placed strategically around the room did little to help.

"Morning captain," I greeted the ops co-ordinator Vark, one of my fellow chopper pilots.

"Howzit Klausie, nothing for you at the moment, but you're on Search and Rescue standby with Paul from 10.00 to 14.00 Bravo. Is the S and R radio serviceable?" I had checked it earlier, but promised to give him a buzz when I got back to the rooms.

After a cup of coffee and a natter, I went back to the pilots' quarters and got into my cozzie and lay down with the S and R radio on the only patch of lawn for hundreds of kilometres around. There was a tiny pool, not much bigger than a big fishpond, that served as a centre point for a lot of the social activity on the base. As the morning wore on the pool area got busier with most of the guys talking shop or reading. Paul arrived and took over the radio. I was Paul's *sandsak* on this bush tour so my job was to follow him around like a puppy dog and do what I was told until I got more experience. There was a lot to learn. In the distance I heard some jets taking off and an Alouette flew high overhead providing top cover for the "Flossie", our name for the C130, bringing troops and supplies from home. It was a quiet day by all accounts, as I lay in the sun thinking about lunch. The Rhodesians had a saying for times like this: "May the war never end." Little did I know that for me it was just about to begin!

The Impala MK 2 was the sharp end of our initiative at Ondangwa, because it could carry a reasonable weapons load and was quite economical to operate for a jet. It had good manoeuvrability when flying low level and was very effective as a ground attack platform. In line with their combat role they also had the highest rate of attrition and we lost quite a number of them. However, thanks to the legendary Martin Baker ejection seat, most of the pilots that ejected from a stricken Imp survived to tell the tale. The search and rescue standby that we did was purely in their honour. They would take off and fly a predetermined route and attack targets on that route. If one got shot down or had a catastrophic failure, the boys in the ops room could pinpoint their position very accurately and the standby S and R Pumas would be despatched to pick the pilot up. The pilots also had emergency locator beacons and flares packed into their kit so it was possible to fly directly to them, even in dense bush, and the "search" part of the equation was simplified.

I took a dip in the pool and played some cards, chatted to the doctors and read a bit and was just settling down for a snooze when the S and R radio crackled next to Paul. "Standby crews to the ops room immediately!" Everyone hushed expecting the worst.

"Get your maps, Nick." Paul was already heading for the room to put on his kit. I did the same and we arrived at the ops room a few minutes later.

"Aubrey Bell has been shot down over Omapanda." Vark glanced at Paul and they both looked very worried.

"Oh shit!" Paul grunted under his breath. I'd never heard of the place.

"Stephan is giving him top cover, but he only has about twenty five minutes left and he is almost out of ammo." Stef was Aubrey's wingman in the two ship Impala recce sortie. "It sounds as if Aubrey ejected and landed close to the camp perimeter, but his plane hit the deck about half a mile away in thick bush and started a bush fire. Stef says there are vehicles from the camp headed towards the wreckage so they don't know where Aubrey is, but it won't take them long to find him."

I found Omapanda on the map. No wonder Vark and Paul looked so worried. It was about twenty kilometres inside Angola just south of a small town called Ongiva, our enemy's version of Ondangwa and the whole area was a network of terrorist camps. It was part of their front line logistic setup, a sort of overnight camp for terrorists moving in and out of Ovamboland.

I quickly worked out our heading and time to target – not too far, about twenty five minutes. I ran out to the chopper. Paul was already strapped in and doing the pre-start checks and the second chopper and crew were also ready to start. Being the lead chopper we carried the troops, a section of twelve ParaBats who were already seated in the back. Their officer, John, looked surprisingly calm and he obviously didn't know what was going on. The tension was infectious and I was becoming very nervous myself. Our job was to pick up Aubrey, using the troops to find him and bring him to the chopper, whilst the second Puma was empty – in case we got shot down – so they could pick up whoever was left.

Huck and Dozy in the other Puma had already started and, once our two engines were started, we did the checks and Paul decided to take off from where we were. The enormous power of the twin turbines lifted the Puma effortlessly and soon we were skimming smoothly over the treetops at close to 250 km per hour.

For a change, the navigation was simple. The main road that led into Angola ran straight past it. After about fifteen minutes of flying over the featureless sand and palm trees, the bush became thicker with a lot of acacia type thorn bushes and the occasional baobab tree, to the point where the sand was only visible around the small African villages that dotted the area. We crossed over the cutline that marked the Angolan border, a line of cleared bush that spread to the left and right as far as the eye could see, and checked our time to target. I need not have bothered, because I could see a thin column of black smoke rising out of the bush on the horizon. My heart started racing and I could feel the lines of sweat running down my face and chest. I was still new at this game, but it didn't take much to figure out this was a bad one.

I called Stef. He was almost out of fuel and had expended all his ammo at the activity around the wreck. He was very agitated. "They have left the plane and are sweeping the bush towards the camp. It won't be long before they find him. His parachute is in a clearing about 50 metres from the west side of the camp, but I can't see him; he must be hiding next to the clearing. I have to go now or I won't make it back. Go for it guys!" We were getting close now and I could see Stef's Impala circling high above the smoke.

"Nice one Stef, see you in the pub." Paul was unbelievably cool given the situation.

The needle on the instrument panel was pointing straight ahead at Aubrey's emergency locator beacon. I turned in my seat to check that John had his radio frequency correctly set and shouted a rundown of what was going on above the noise. He got very excited and looked like a pitbull terrier straining at his leash. He barked a command over his shoulder and I heard the clatter of magazines and rifles loading in the back. I flicked the undercarriage lever down and did the landing checks.

In the distance, I could see the parachute lying in the clearing and as we got closer the line of trenches marking the edge of the camp came into view. What I saw next was horrifying. Streams of gooks were running towards our side of the camp. They had obviously realised where we were going to land and they knew where Alan was lying. I heard a strange sound above the noise of the chopper, a sort of irregular 'pok', 'pok', 'pok' and I realised we were being shot at and the bullets were hitting the chopper. It was getting more intense by the second.

We landed with a thump next to the chute, the doors flew open and John and his men were out in an instant. Paul took off immediately, powered over the trees and banked hard right over the camp, flying very low. The gooks were firing at us with AKs, and the equipment and trenches were littered everywhere. Luckily for us they seemed to be totally disorganised.

"We found him, he's injured!" John's voice crackled, the background noise on the radio was thick with gunfire and men shouting. By now we were a few hundred metres south of the camp and we turned in for the approach, bracing ourselves for the pickup. We started to slow down as the chute came into view again.

As we approached the chute I realised we had a serious problem. The firefight between the ParaBats and the enemy was taking place over the area around the chute and we had to land between them! The whole clearing was a cloud of dust and smoke caused by the choppers downwash and the rifle fire, with flashes of tracer and smoke trails from rocket-propelled grenades criss-crossing in front of us. I looked at Paul, but he was ahead of me, his eyes scanning desperately for an alternative place to land. There was none, the thick bush made that impossible, and if we landed too far away we could lose the ParaBats and that spelt disaster. We had no choice but to take the hammering, so in we went!

When we landed, the shooting from the camp became frenzied and the ParaBats stopped firing completely. We were all sitting ducks. Then, to my amazement the ParaBats came out of the bush on the left like lightning, ran past the chopper and positioned themselves between us and the enemy and started shooting again. This was a masterstroke and indicated clear thinking under incredible pressure. The enemy must have thought the ParaBats were going to take them on in the camp because a lot of them got up and ran away from the fight, some of them falling in the hail of bullets. John appeared out of the bush with Aubrey hanging onto him, his left leg hanging limply and no doubt broken from when he landed after ejecting. Sieg, our engineer, pulled Aubrey aboard and in a flash the ParaBats turned and piled in. John was last in after checking he had all his men.

We took off and then made a big mistake. Paul turned right again, over the camp, and we copped it big time. We heard deeper and more ominous bangs. They were firing anti-aircraft guns at us as well as all the other stuff. Suddenly, there was a sharp thud and Paul's head whipped back as the cockpit was showered with splinters of glass. The nose dipped sharply and the ground came up fast. Instinctively I grabbed the cyclic and pulled the nose up, missing the ground by a whisker and ploughing the leaves off the top of a tree as we leapt upwards, the Puma shuddering as it clawed for air.

Just then, one of the ParaBats crumpled over howling with pain. He had taken a bullet through the thigh and forearm as he sat on the chopper floor. John was there immediately, tearing at his first aid kit. I glanced at Paul, and to my relief saw that he was okay apart from a cut above his right eye. He took back control of the aircraft and the shooting faded as we flew clear of the camp.

I heard Huck in the other chopper calling. "There's smoke coming from underneath your aircraft." There was a strong smell of fuel, but no burning. There were so many bullet holes in the fuel tanks that the leaking fuel looked like smoke in our Puma's slipstream.

We now had two wounded in the back and had to go to the hospital at Oshakati first. I watched the fuel gauges falling for a while and guessed we had about thirty minutes fuel left. A big chopper like the Puma is very thirsty and burns tons of fuel in a day's work, so fuel tanks full of holes were bad news. Paul told Huck to follow us in case we had to land in a hurry, so that they could finish the job.

We landed at Oshakati and shut down the engines so that the doctors and medics could work on the two wounded guys. I stood next to the chopper for a while, checking out the bullet holes that pock-marked just about every part of the aircraft and watched the fuel pouring onto the helipad like a garden waterfall. It occurred to me how lucky we had been and that no one had been killed. Paul had had a very close shave with the bullet that came through the front windscreen; it missed his right temple by a fraction and passed through the bulkhead behind his head. I felt strangely numb and detached from the whole thing, as if it were a dream. I suppose the massive adrenaline rush had worn off and a kind of shock had set in.

An ambulance took Aubrey and the wounded ParaBat away. I figured the Puma must have been just about drained empty and wondered how we were going to get back to Ondangwa. By road no doubt?

Paul hoisted himself into his seat and started strapping in. "What about the fuel, major?" I asked.

"Fuck that, we'll make it, and anyway I'm thirsty." He appeared totally unfazed by the whole incident. Obviously fear was not on his list of emotions.

We landed at Ondangwa, which was only six minutes flying time, with the fuel gauges on zero. A large group of our mates and military personnel had gathered and we were literally carried out of the chopper to cheering and applause. I had a beer stuck in my hand and guys slapping me on the back. This had been an amazing outcome given the odds and I suppose we had good reason to celebrate. There was a heck of a party in the pub that night and we all got up late the next day.

Huck's chopper had also taken a pasting, although not as bad as ours, but they got hit by a 23mm anti-aircraft bullet that blew a big hole in the rear fuselage. Luckily nobody had been injured.

Later the following morning, I wandered up to the hardstand to look at our choppers and was surprised to find them already stripped, covered with canvas and loaded into a C130 ready to go back to the States for repairs. Sieg showed me two badly distorted bullets he had taken out of the fuel tanks. They were AK47 tracers. The Puma has bladder tanks made out of rubber that have no air in them, if not for this we would have exploded in mid air. Again I counted my blessings. We had almost 200 holes and by some miracle none of the essential parts like the engines, gearboxes and hydraulics had been hit.

The commanding officer of Ondangwa, Major Baz, was standing nearby talking to the C130 crew. He called me over. "So cocksparrow, Pine tells me your flying kit is not up to scratch." I thought I was in trouble again. "There's some old kit in my office, just help yourself and consider yourself shat on." I guess it was his way of showing me I was earning my stripes.

Paul and John, as well as five of John's troopies subsequently received the Honoris Crux, our nation's highest award for bravery and the rest of us got commendation medals. It was good to be acknowledged for something like that. I would have given every single one of those ParaBats an HC. Damn they were good and all just teenagers doing National Service! They were an absolute credit to the youth of our country and, again, a testament to the high standard of training we received in those days.

11
The Lion and the Elephant

"Don't go too close dear, them things bite"
Dulcie Savage

Brute was a deceptive name for one of my best friends in the Air Force. He was an immediately likeable person, quiet and mild mannered with a spontaneous sense of humour. I flew many hours as his co-pilot on Pumas and enjoyed his patient style. He was quick to praise and firm when correcting mistakes, never raising his voice and always explaining and demonstrating what he required. He always treated me as an equal.

We did a bush tour in a place called Mpacha, which was the main airfield of the Eastern Caprivi. The Caprivi Strip forms the northern boundary of the Chobe Delta, a huge network of swamps and rivers that feeds into the Zambezi River and flows over the Victoria Falls, a hundred or so kilometres downstream. Due to the war, poachers and hunters kept well clear of the area and as a result, the game flourished to the point where it was acknowledged as having the highest game count in Africa. As a pristine African reserve it's got the works: no fences and power lines, very few roads and dense bush made up of African hardwoods, surrounded by meandering savannah filled with elephant grass, higher than your head that is almost impossible to walk through. The rivers and swamps are crystal clear, filtered by millions of acres of papyrus reeds and in more recent times, they have been used by scuba diving film crews making wildlife documentaries, presumably because they can film crocs and hippos at a safe distance in near perfect conditions. Every species of African animal thrives, including rare species such as the Red Lechwe – a rare swamp antelope.

One day Brute, Bones our engineer and myself were briefed to take an evaluation team to Fort Doppies, a recce training camp deep in the bush that no-one was supposed to know about. We took off after breakfast and headed west for about thirty minutes to a camp that was quite close to where I did my border tour during National Service. As we skimmed over the treetops, my thoughts went back to the time I had spent at Sifuma and because we did foot patrols for three days at a time, I got to know the bush quite well. I could go on for many pages recounting the experiences we had with wild animals, such as finding elephant tracks in our temporary camp one morning. To this day I wonder if an elephant did not walk through the camp while we were sleeping. Hyenas surrounded us at night and we shot into the bush to scare them off and one day we even came across a pride of lions that showed absolutely no interest in us. On one occasion we watched fish eagles glide gracefully over the river and pluck fish out of the water. We heard stories of soldiers who had disappeared silently without a trace near the river, taken by a crocodile; the only clue a bit of his kit lying near the water's edge and within shouting distance of his mates.

We did an orbit around the camp and landed. We were greeted by Sergeant Major Kobus van Wyk, a seasoned professional soldier and instructor with the Reconnaissance Corps, the South African equivalent of the SAS. The visitors knew their way around and made off in a *gharry*, whilst Kobus offered to show Brute, Bones and me around the camp.

Over a cup of coffee we learned that the camp was only occupied about half the time and so, with time on his hands, Kobus had become involved with the nature conservation officials in the area, taking a keen interest in their work.

He told us about his love for lions and took us to see two cubs that had been orphaned a few weeks earlier. According to Kobus their mother had been injured in a hunt and had been cornered by a pack of hyenas. She fought for hours to defend her cubs but the hyenas wore her down and killed her. Kobus had found the cubs under a tree trunk close to her remains. The rivalry between lions and hyenas is fierce, as both of them are formidable predators. Hyenas will never hesitate to kill a vulnerable lion and lionesses spend the first few weeks alone with their newborn cubs, until they are strong enough to join the pride.

Kobus had tried to raise cubs before with limited success. He had the support of the local rangers, but cubs have to be taught how to hunt by their mother and don't stand a chance in the wild without these skills. An orphaned lion's best hope of survival is in a zoo or a game park where their environment is controlled. Hand-raised lions can be fully-grown and yet be killed by wild lions that sense their vulnerability. Also, without their mother's milk to build up their immunity, they are prone to sickness and don't last long anyway.

We came to an enclosure about the size of a double garage that was normally used for police dogs and found the two cubs. They were full of fun, resembling

Presented with pilots' wings by Chief of the Air Force, Lt. General Bob Rogers. November 1978. (Author's Collection)

Fellow Candidate Officer Theo Scheepers and the author wearing their new uniforms and 'Candidate Officer' stripes. Skip also wears the SADF parachute qualification wings. (Author's Collection)

The Harvard – treated reverently by pilots under training, the 'Spam Can' had an uncanny knack for biting unwary students! (Lt. Colonel William Marshall SANDF)

The Impala – 'A fine trainer; skimming over the trees at 550km/hour and navigating off a hand-held map'. (Lt. Colonel William Marshall SANDF)

Helicopter Operational Training Course – AFB Bloemspruit 1979. Rear row - Nick Lithgow – Mike Lomberg – Pete Francey – Steve Joubert – Andy Crawford – Simon Hearn – Stevie Erasmus – Brian Bell; Front row - Danie Terblanche – Kevin Reynolds – Floppy Laatz – Thys Carstens – Arthur Bradstreet – Billy Fourie – Paul Downer – Brian King. (Author's Collection)

The author takes off from Sclanders Farm on a mountain flying sortie. (Author's Collection)

The ubiquitous and highly versatile Alouette on operations in Angola – agile and adaptable; from gunship to casevac, these aircraft were the SADF's Light Cavalry. (Jim Hooper)

The Aérospatiale SA 330 Puma – rugged and reliable – an emperor amongst medium lift helicopters. (SANDF Archives)

'Casevac!' – Injured servicemen are handed into the care of the SAMS. The SADF field hospitals were excellent. Many were staffed by highly trained medical professionals routed into the military through National Service. (SANDF Archives)

Pumas in formation low over the bush, a 'troopie' looks on anxiously. The bush war took its toll on both machine and man. Few in the 'States' were aware of the war's intensity. (SANDF Archives)

Troopies prepare to emplane Pumas in the 'Operational Area' - headgear removed, equipment fastened, antennas collapsed and weapons 'made safe'. (SANDF Archives)

An Alouette flight engineer monitors the tail rotor for hazards as the aircraft clears yet another 'Operational Area' LZ. (Jim Hooper)

'Smoke on!' An Alouette hurtles to an LZ marked by Signal Smoke Yellow. The density of the 'Operational Area' bush is obvious. Trees and bush were a constant operating hazard. (Jim Hooper)

Yet another casevac – an injured 'troopie' is extracted by an SAAF Alouette. Many lives were saved by the SAAF's timely airmanship. (Jim Hooper)

ParaBats next to a Puma and C160 Transall aircraft at Ondangwa. The SAAF aircrew had a grudging respect for these elite paratroopers. (SANDF Archives)

Into the setting sun – Pumas hug the lie of the land during Operation Uric. (SANDF Archives)

domestic kittens in mentality, but were about three times the size of a fully-grown cat and their teeth and claws commanded great respect.

Kobus then told us about Teddy, a fifteen month-old lion he had raised from a few weeks old and his greatest success so far. Teddy had become too big to live in the camp and besides terrifying the staff, he needed over twenty kilograms of fresh meat a day. So he was moved to another camp close to the river that was used by the troops for recreation. Teddy was clearly very close to Kobus' heart and for a man not prone to emotion, he was absolutely sparkling with enthusiasm when he suggested we pay his lion a visit.

We set off on a sand track through the pristine bush, the old *gharry* creaking and lurching through the thick sand that was not negotiable without four wheel drive. I sat in the back with Bones as memories of this area from my National Service flooded back. The air was still and thick with heat that drained all our energy. The bush was packed with wildlife. A herd of impalas watched us nervously from the fringes of a thickly wooded area as we crawled along the edge of an elephant grass *shonna*. We saw kudu, sable, waterbuck and a herd of buffalos within ten minutes. Dozens of vultures circled in the thermals overhead and we passed a herd of elephants standing under a large tree fanning themselves with their ears. Eventually, we came to a large opening next to a river and stopped to watch a herd of hundreds of Lechwe antelopes crossing the gap between two islands. They cascaded gracefully into the river, four abreast, swimming with surprising speed, emerging like a giant yellow snake from the foam of splashing water and disappearing into the bush, perfectly camouflaged in the shadows.

We stopped in the middle of the opening and got out, not venturing too far from the *gharry*. Kobus walked into a shady area nearby and I noticed the recreation area for the first time. A large stone *braai* surrounded by hardwood tables and benches stood in a clearing under the trees; a good place for fishing and a few beers with your mates. He was calling Teddy as you would call a dog and soon Kobus emerged walking briskly towards us, looking rather nervously over his shoulder. In the shadows behind him something was following. When Kobus reached us, Teddy emerged into the sunlight and an overwhelming feeling of fear and excitement came over me. Cold shivers ran down my spine as all my alarm bells rang! He padded towards us and stopped about three metres away eyeing us curiously. He was enormous, his shoulders about the height of my hips and paws that could tear you in half with one swipe. Teddy was at once the most fearsome and beautiful creature I have ever seen. Kobus told us to stand still and Teddy would greet us one at a time. He knew Kobus was no threat and rubbed his muzzle on Kobus' belly and then moved on to me. Before he muzzled me, he looked up for a second and I was struck by the gold colour of his eyes and sensed a primal intelligence, fearlessness and a casual familiarity with death.

At fifteen months old, he was on the threshold of maturity and still had light spots on his fur and the start of what would become a very impressive mane. As he moved on to Bones he rubbed the length of his body along my hips. As scared as I was I could not resist putting my hand on his back, feeling the thick dusty fur and noticing his strong natural smell. He stopped short of Bones eyeing him suspiciously and moved straight on to Brute, ignoring Bones with typical feline arrogance. Kobus told Bones to get back into the *gharry* as Teddy obviously didn't like him and Bones moved stiffly away, no doubt very relieved. After greeting Brute, he loped off to the river and started drinking, again just like a domestic cat. We watched him for a while and even although he was twenty metres away, I still felt very exposed.

Kobus said he wanted to play with him, so we climbed onto the back of the *gharry* and let the two good friends enjoy each other's company. Teddy started getting rough after a while and I could see Kobus was reading the signals. A playful swipe from one of those paws could put him in hospital and he strategically manoeuvred his way back into the driver's seat. Before we left, Kobus chased him around with the *gharry* for a while and when we turned away, he was left standing in the opening looking mournfully after us. And so ended the most awesome experience I have ever had with an animal.

Kobus explained how he had tried in vain to teach Teddy to hunt by dragging a buck carcass behind the *bakkie*. It was all just fun and games to Teddy and very little was achieved, so as long as he lived he would be dependent on humans for survival.

On the way back to the main camp we stopped frequently to admire the animals. When we got to the big tree where we had seen the elephants earlier they were gone, but Kobus stopped a bit further down the track and looked intensely into the thick bush. He whispered that the elephants were close by and asked if we wanted to see them close up. Brute and I nodded, but Bones was less keen as Teddy's snub was still fresh in his mind and he decided not to push his luck. Kobus signalled for me to follow close behind and told Brute to wait. We walked slowly into the bush, Kobus hesitating occasionally as he stared ahead into the shadows. The tension was mounting inside me again. We stopped and stood dead still for what seemed like ages and then he reached back slowly, putting his arm around my shoulders and pulling me closer. Ahead of us was nothing but trees and shadows and I was beginning to wonder what all the fuss was about when I saw it. Kobus must have felt my body jerk in shock because he tightened his grip and held me firm. I wanted to run. To my astonishment an elephant was standing no more than ten paces away, so perfect was her camouflage and not too far behind her, stood about a dozen of them which I also had not seen. We stood there for a minute savouring the magic as I admired the wrinkled texture of her skin and her tusks, the nails on her gigantic feet and her ears and trunk swaying gently back and forth.

Kobus took a step back and slowly we retreated to the *gharry* keeping our eyes on the elephant, just in case. Wild animals are unpredictable at the best of times, but she seemed at ease and even comfortable with our presence. This to my mind was proof of the low level of exposure that the animals in this area had to humans, as well as the absence of hunters and poachers.

Brute was very amused at the expression I had on my face as he and Kobus disappeared into the bush to enjoy the experience. Brute told me later that the elephant started to move off while they were watching and didn't make a sound. Not the crack of a twig or the rustle of leaves.

Back at the camp we had a light lunch, stunned and amazed by the incredible experience. We speculated on why Teddy had reacted so strangely to Bones and decided it must have been the smell of oil and chemicals on his flying overalls that had upset him, as Bones was responsible for all the maintenance on the Puma. When the visitors heard about our experience they demanded that Kobus give them a tour, which he promised to do next time round.

On the flight back to Mpacha I found myself searching the bush below us for signs of animals and seeing the bush from the air now had a whole new meaning. The experience had reignited a passion and awareness that has never faded.

12

The Landmine

"Slay them all – God will know which are His"
Abbé de Citeaux

"You have good days and bad days." Peanuts smiled wryly as I swilled the last of a very greasy military breakfast down with a glass of chilled orange juice. He must have been looking at the expression on my face because I knew I would have heartburn until lunchtime. He had many such phrases that he used to illustrate the ups and downs of daily life, and he offered them with a casual indifference that never failed to get a smile or a laugh.

As we strolled back to the ops room I had a bit of time to think about this place. All the other crews were already flying, but we were on casevac standby so we had the rare luxury of getting up late and enjoying an unrushed breakfast. This was my third bush tour and I knew from experience that it would not be long before we were called out.

It was stinking hot outside, overcast and humid. The whole of Ondangwa had been awash for the last twelve hours from a storm that had raged throughout the night. This left the whole camp covered with large pools of muddy water which had to be negotiated with particular care, especially at night on the way back from the pub. Anything that needed to be kept dry was raised slightly above the normal ground level, like the roads, runway, hangars, stores and clinic, and of course the ops room which was the crossroads for virtually all the activity on the base. Anything that was not thoughtfully engineered was flooded every day in summer by ferocious thunderstorms.

We lived in small prefabricated fibreboard houses mounted on short brick pillars called "terrapins". In our case, they were allocated according to aircraft type, so on very rare occasions when the healthy rivalry that existed between us soured, a mini war broke out between, for instance, between the chopper terrapin and the jet jockey terrapin. On one particularly disturbing occasion a *vlammie* flicked a cigarette end into the chopper quarters, possibly by accident. This did not pass unnoticed and was replied to with an apple core. An empty beer can was answered with a tea cup which led to an aluminium pot and a chunk of watermelon, a tin of curry and a stale half loaf being slung across the gap. The situation continued to deteriorate until finally a phosphorous grenade was tossed into the jet jockeys' room. This exploded a split second after the panic-stricken pilots had leapt out of the windows and doors. It razed the place in a few minutes taking all their equipment and personal belongings with it.

As the camp matured in later years the terrapins were replaced with brick buildings that were a lot more spacious and comfortable. They also offered better protection against the occasional mortar attack.

At the ops room we made a cup of coffee and chatted to the staff busy with the task of running a war. The banks of radios crackled and hissed as information passed to and from the dozen or so aircraft flying out there somewhere. Occasionally I recognized a voice, but I could not figure out where they were or what they were doing. We were trained to speak cryptically on the radio, never using the names of people, places or aircraft, even to the point of not saying yes or no but leaving a blank space, using slang or simply a click on the transmitter that answered by implication. We sort of spoke a language within a language and surprisingly this seldom led to confusion. If the enemy were listening in, the radio chatter would have been meaningless. The problem was that we tended to take this language home with us and friends and family would end up totally confused by what we would consider a normal conversation. A typical sentence would go like this. "Hocks Ballas, can we scale your *gharry* to *klap* some tubes for the *braai*?" the answer would be "Ja, *klap* it cock." Figure that one out!?

As I suspected, we did not have to wait long for a call out. A call came through from Oshakati about a landmine explosion. I hated these casevacs because it always upset me to see our own troops injured. It was on a road about forty kilometres east of us and a truck was involved. This was stating the obvious as all of the military vehicles in the area were trucks of some description. Being on a road it would be easy to find. The whole area was a web of tracks through the bush, but in summer most of the traffic kept to the roads which were built above the storm water line. This unfortunately made the disgusting job of laying landmines very easy for the enemy who used the puddles of water and loose sand as camouflage. Laying an anti-tank mine in these conditions only took a few seconds.

I found the spot on my map and walked out to the Puma to start the pre-flight routine. Peanuts was strapping in whilst Botter, our engineer, was helping the doctor and his two medics organize their gear in the back and within a few minutes we were ready to go. The rotors winding up to full rpm accompanied by the whine of the turbines was becoming very familiar by now, something we did at least half a dozen times a day. The Puma was a complex chopper and there were a fair number of checks that had to be done. We shared the workload between the three of us with me doing the radio and the navigation, Peanuts flying and Botter monitoring the systems. Soon we were cruising across the treetops under the gloomy sky, occasionally flying through patches of rain and dodging flocks of birds that were too slow to get out of our way. Where the millions of birds came from in this soggy sandscape never ceased to amaze me.

Navigation could be difficult at low level, which was seldom more than seventy feet above the ground, because the whole area for hundreds of kilometres around Ondangwa was as flat as a pancake, with only the bush changing in composition from pans of water and palm trees, to thick thorn bush. This carried through deep into Angola where we had to use hand drawn maps in certain areas, and most navigation was done on heading and time. Later on, after many hours of flying in this area, I found I instinctively knew where to go and rarely used maps.

We intercepted the road at a shallow angle and turned to follow its line, which was straight as far ahead as the eye could see. After a while, I noticed a crowd of people looking like ants on the road, far in the distance. As we got closer I made out a number of military vehicles scattered around the site but I could not see the truck that had hit the landmine. We did an orbit over the area, Peanuts chose a flat spot close to the road to land on and we turned onto the approach. I put the undercarriage down, did the landing checks and looked out at the scene before me.

After we landed I began to grasp the horror of what had happened. The reason I didn't spot the damaged vehicle was because it had been blown to pieces. Parts of it lay strewn over a large area and the only evidence that it once existed was a crumpled piece of chassis with the remains of the tray and a spring attached to it. A crater that could swallow a car marked the spot on the road where the landmine had been placed. As it turned out, the vehicle was a civilian truck that was carrying a large family, probably on their way back from the market judging by the cans of food and bags of meal that littered the area. We found out later that three mines had been placed on top of each other, explaining why the explosion had been so devastating, an old trick that never failed to impress, but they had been detonated by the wrong target. Instead of one of our army vehicles, the bastards had blown up a truck full of their own people.

The medics piled their gear and stretchers up next to us on a dry patch of grass as Peanuts and an Army officer shouted to each other above the noise of the chopper. We needed another Puma as there were fifteen dead and injured and the whole lot had to go to the hospital at Oshakati. The Army officer asked us not to shut down, so we sat there with the engines at ground idle and I called ops on the long wave radio and asked for another aircraft. We were lucky, Steel and Roy were in an empty chopper on their way back to Ondangwa and they had enough fuel to help us out.

Within a minute, the first stretchers arrived with the wounded. A grey-haired old man unconscious and spattered with blood was the first in. Then a teenage girl, maybe sixteen years old with her eyes rolling in terror and a hand missing, followed by a young man whose body was dreadfully mutilated and clothed in little more than shredded, blood-sodden rags. His eyes and nose had been mowed away by a jagged object and his legs were twisted like knots.

They kept coming and I tried not to look anymore, shocked out of my wits by this soulless horror. There was nowhere to look without witnessing pain, gross mutilation and death. Then I noticed something that riveted my attention. What looked like a child was sitting in the middle of the road, with his little head and shoulders hunched over in a prayer-like position. At this distance, it looked as if he was playing with a toy and my first impulse was to get him off the road. Then a soldier walked up to him, picked him up by the ankle and unceremoniously dumped his limp body head first into a black plastic bag.

These terrible images remain with me to this day.

After a few minutes we had all six of the survivors in our chopper. A grim faced Botter advanced the fuel flow levers and I did the take-off checks. We took off and set a heading for Oshakati as the other Puma was quite close, but there was no rush for them. All they had to do was pick up the remaining bodies.

In the back, the doctor and medics were working furiously and the whole floor was littered with people, bloody bandages, syringes and empty vials. Drips were being hung from every available spot and the Puma stank of blood, disinfectant, faeces and fear.

We flew in silence. After a while the radio mast at Shacks appeared on the horizon and we headed for the landing pad. Again there was no need to shut down as the transfer of patients to the camo coloured ambulances went quickly and we headed back to Ondangwa after a few minutes. The mess in the back was unbelievable. The doctor and his team were smeared with blood as they tidied up, blank ashen expressions fixed on their faces. This was a bad one, even for them.

Back at Ondangwa I had a swim and some lunch and laid down for a snooze, but nothing could stop the ghastly images from going round and round in my mind. For the first time I wondered what the whole damn war was about, or what any war was about for that matter. The enemy seemed indifferent as to whom they murdered; whether it was us or their own people meant nothing to them. For a long time after that incident I had to remind myself why I joined the Air Force. I wanted to fly, and the training, equipment and experience in the SAAF was only available to a chosen few. It was an honour and a privilege to fly at that level, and besides that, I had a job to do. But these convictions did little to ease the doubt and confusion that weighed on my conscience.

Back in our terrapin, Peanuts was sitting silently at a table flicking some playing cards through his fingers with the deftness of a seasoned gambler, the familiar fag hanging from the corner of his lips. He had a habit of lifting his eyebrows and squinting his eyes against the smoke and when he looked at me I knew he was trying to measure my reaction to the day's events. He had many years experience and had also been through this when he was a junior pilot. I tried to give nothing away.

" … you OK Klausie?"

"Yea, I'm fine major"

"Ja … you have good days and bad days," he drawled in a husky voice. Take it on the chin and get on with your job. There was no other way forward I guess.

13
The Bush Formal

"Whiskey has killed more men than bullets, but most men would rather be full of whiskey than bullets"
Logan Pearsall Smith

On average we were spending a month in the bush and two weeks at home, which had advantages and disadvantages. The biggest disadvantage was not being able to develop a serious relationship with a girlfriend, but in this respect both Jim and I were lucky. Jim was going great guns with Sandy and I had a sneaking suspicion that they would get married. Jiggs, despite his crazy attitude to life, was quite grounded in some respects and he had no doubts that he wanted to be an airline pilot and that the SAAF was a short to medium term arrangement, which would give him the hours and experience he would need to get a good job in commercial aviation.

Because we were so busy, the time passed quickly and it was not long before I had the required flying hours on the Puma to become a commander. I hitched a lift on the old Viscount from Durbs up to Swartkops and started preparing for my test. Most of the test was instrument flying which we did very little of in normal operations. The last time I did all the exercises was during the conversion, so a fair amount of spit and polish was needed. I reported back to 19B a few days later with my Puma command in hand. The transition from co-pilot to commander was not that dramatic on the Puma because all the flying was shared 50/50, but it's always nice to take another step up the ladder.

Another thing that became glaringly obvious was that this job, besides being an incredible adventure and very rewarding, was bloody dangerous, and becoming more so as the enemy got more support from Russia and Cuba. There were rumours of radar stations being set up in Angola and the sophisticated weapon systems they used were being found a lot closer to the border. It was all very well flying this great chopper and getting in the hours that would be unimaginable in civvy street, but you were constantly putting your life on the line. In all the time I had been going to Ondangwa, no chopper pilots had been lost and it seemed to be the Imp pilots taking most of the flak with two of them shot down and killed, but it was only a matter of time. Another thing we had to contend with more and more was the lack of spares for the choppers. I had two non-combat related engine failures, one where the engine exploded, and both these failures indicated we were pushing the limits of serviceability. The cost of overhauling the engines was astronomical and because of sanctions, the engines, and indeed most of the parts, were irreplaceable. We were constantly reminded of the need to look after the aircraft. There were no restrictions on our flying hours, but this was to be the next step. We easily flew a hundred hours a month in the bush and thirty on the squadron, so the wear and tear on the choppers was substantial.

I arrived at Ondangwa for a tour when I was told that Major Baz had been replaced, which was a pity because he was very popular and it was hard to imagine the base without him. The reason was because his wife was suffering from stress. Quite understandable too, having to live in a war zone with few friends and very limited facilities. His replacement was Commandant van de Kuip, whom I had not met before, but had heard he had a reputation as a stickler for cleanliness and discipline. He was a transport pilot who had flown Daks and Hercules and he had arrived, with both his wife and mother-in-law, to command the base for a year.

While I was clearing in, I saw him sitting in his office and decided to introduce myself and get the formality out of the way. I knocked on his door and went in when he responded, giving him a salute. I waited for him to stand and shake my hand, as was the custom. But he just sat behind his desk and stared at me.

"*Fokken* chopper pilot, eh?" he said finally, glancing at the badges on my flying overalls. He spoke rapidly, almost stuttering, and it was obvious from his accent that he spoke very little English. "*En Engels nogal!*" he cursed under his breath. I sensed a deeply rooted mistrust, probably going back to the Boer War some eighty years earlier, although his eyes had a strangely mischievous twinkle. He stood up slowly, his tall thin frame towering over me, and put a nicotine-stained claw forward in greeting. But when I took his hand he used the grip to pull me closer, to the point where I had to lean on his desk to keep my balance. "Jus' watch *jou fokken* step *voeltjie*," he hissed in my ear. "*Ek vat nie kak van julle bliksems,*" giving me a wicked grin, so close I could see the network of veins on his nose and the yellow streaks on his teeth. If I did not know better, he was looking forward to our first confrontation.

This over, I backed out through the door and took a big breath of fresh air when I got outside. In my haste to escape, I almost fell over Mick, who was waiting his turn. I must have had a funny expression on my face, because he commented, "Ah, you've just met the Vertical Cockroach," he chuckled knowingly.

Later we heard that VC wanted to hold a dinner to welcome himself to Ondangwa and the date was set for the following Saturday night. Extra rations of steak were ordered from Grootfontein and countless bottles of sherry, port, red and white wine were ordered from the pub. The sherry and port indicated that the meal was to be in the mould of a formal dinner and our browns were to be clean, ironed and adorned with rank. It was a busy week so Saturday came quickly. Early that evening, we decided to have a few beers in the pub before supper. We were getting ready to drive down to the mess, when Buddy, one of the Alouette gunship pilots, produced a bottle of Galliano and a dozen beers, so we decided to have a drink in the rooms first. Now Galliano is one of those deceptive drinks that looks and tastes like a cool drink, but kicks like a mule. When mixed with anything else it has a very fast acting effect. I had never drunk the stuff before and when Brute saw me eyeing the bottle he warned me to watch it. We had a beer and a Galliano each and then all piled into the *gharry*, heading for the mess. Buddy said he had a few things to do and he would walk down later.

The pub at Ondangwa had the distinction of having the longest bar in South West Africa. It was about fifteen metres long and made of kiaat, a beautiful two-toned hardwood. It was curved at one end to create a corner with the wall which was known famously as "Chopper Corner". The pub was packed. All the officers and most of the NCOs on the base were invited, plus a contingent of officers from Oshakati.

The atmosphere was very festive, everybody was relaxed and for a few hours the war was all but forgotten. The chef came in from the kitchen and had a chat and a beer with VC, whilst a few waiters wandered around with trays of sherry glasses which we pretended to sip delicately. Then we all filed into the mess hall and I was pleased to see the tables had been laid out informally, a departure from the usual U shape, and that you could sit anywhere you wanted.

Then I blundered badly. I noticed that Buddy was missing and it occurred to me that maybe he had lost track of time. I decided to fetch him from the rooms, so I got the keys for the *gharry* and went back outside. I had just climbed into the *gharry* when I saw him walking through the buildings to the mess. "Come on hurry up, the guys are sitting down already." I walked back into the hall with Buddy behind me and then realized I had blown it. The chopper table was full and the only seats left were between VC, his wife and his mother-in-law. It was going to be one of those evenings.

We made our way over to their table and stood behind our seats waiting for the Dominee to say grace. Then I noticed something strange about Buddy. He was swaying gently, even though he was holding onto the back of the seat, and his eyes were glazed. This was the worst possible place for him to be seated. That Galliano must have been strong because in less than an hour he was rat shit. At the chopper table we would have been able to cover for him, but it was too late now and to make it even worse, he was known to become quite boisterous when drunk.

Buddy was seated next to VC's wife with me opposite him. There was a lot of noise coming from the chopper table on the other side of the room and I noted, with mild surprise, that the Dominee was seated there.

The starters went without incident and I was chatting pleasantly with the mother-in-law when the main course arrived with a few bottles of red wine. The steaks were really good and we had a choice of pepper or garlic butter sauce. Buddy grabbed the pepper sauce bowl and emptied the whole thing onto his plate, which raised the eyebrows of VC's wife, and then I could see him eyeing the bottles. I quickly took our bottle and filled the people's glasses around me, deliberately leaving Buddy out, but when I was finished he grabbed the neck of the bottle and started a tug of war with me. He had this look of drunken determination in his eyes, so before the wine got spilled all over the table, I reluctantly filled his glass. That's when VC first clicked that Buddy was out of it.

"Hey chopper pilot, behave yourself!" He could not remember Buddy's name.

"Shoppa plite *se moer,*" he slurred. "Mynhame… ish… *kokarot,* ha, ha, ha," then took another slug of wine. His head rolled slowly around a few times and then he fell face first into his plate of steak and sauce, spilling his wine all over the table. He had passed out – stone cold.

We all stared at him in disbelief. After what seemed like ages, I realized he couldn't breathe, so I grabbed him by the hair and twisted his head sideways. He lay there with his whole face smeared with gravy and a piece of mushroom stuck in his nose that rattled noisily when he exhaled. VC and his family were dumbstruck at this appalling behaviour and even I, hardened to chopper antics, was shocked.

Brute came to the rescue and together we hauled him back to the *gharry*, amid howls of laughter, leaving him comatose on the back seat. The real danger now was that this incident had set the mood for the evening and when we went back into the mess, I sensed the atmosphere had deteriorated. When I sat down again VC tapped a spoon on his glass and stood up with a very pale and serious expression on his face, looking much like a dehydrated vampire. He had sensed the danger as well.

"I just want to warn all you guys" he said in perfect Afrikaans, "I expect the best behaviour from all of you and that any misdemeanours will be dealt with severely." He then pointed a long thin finger at the chopper table. "And the pilots at that table are on short finals. *Pasop!*" We all started laughing, but VC was serious and looked more than a little worried. He had been in the Air Force a long time and knew what he was dealing with. Buddy's performance was nothing short of disgusting, but VC's wife and mother-in-law had weathered it well, so we continued the meal with smiles and pleasantries. During dessert, I was chatting to the mother-in-law and things seemed to have settled down a little, when suddenly there was a splat, like an egg breaking and her head jerked sideways. I asked her if she was okay and when she turned to me she had a roll packed with butter stuck on the side of her head. It was obviously meant for me, but had missed and hit the worst possible target, apart from VC that is.

Then it started. In a split second, the whole room became a hail of rolls and butter. VC stood up and shouted for order, but it was too late. He got hit a good half dozen times before he grabbed his two companions and fled.

Outside we discovered our *gharry* was missing and we guessed from the occasional serpentine tyre marks carved into the revetments that Buddy had taken it back to the rooms, so we walked back on the road laughing and joking like a bunch of school kids in the Ovambo moonlight.

When we got to the pilots' quarters, there was another surprise waiting. Buddy was on the roof of the jet jockeys' room with, unbelievably, the lawn mower. When he saw us arrive he started cranking furiously, with all of us watching and cheering him on. He was still so drunk that it took quite a few pulls to get the thing fired up, but eventually it chugged into life and he proceeded to "mow" the corrugated iron roof, pushing it back and forward with sparks flying everywhere and making a terrible noise. Then the jet jockeys started getting upset; obviously the roof was going to leak like hell when it rained, and they all started shouting abuse at him. He then pushed the mower precariously close to the edge where it hovered briefly, with two wheels on the roof and Buddy holding the handle, before the whole lot crashed into the ground in a cloud of dust. How he did not injure himself is incredible, but we picked him up and he stood there staring at the bent mower shaking his head, noticeably more sober.

We packed him off to bed, and in a few minutes everything had settled down. We made a fire and sat around chatting and after a while, most of the guys had gone to bed. Jim, Brute and I were left staring at the embers.

Then I noticed Buddy walking shakily over to the fridge. He opened the door and peered inside, supposedly looking for water. But he took out a watermelon and put it on the table. He was hungry and thirsty, so it was a good choice. I was about to call him to join us but he disappeared into the room again and emerged with his flying knife and something else in his other hand. He fiddled about with the melon a bit and then strolled unsteadily over to the jet jockeys room. At the door, he fiddled with the melon again and then rolled it into the room. A few seconds later there was a big bang, followed by howls from the pilots inside. Buddy staggered back to his room killing himself laughing.

When the jet jockeys switched on the light, the whole room was spattered pink and they had a total sense of humour failure. Of course, when they emerged from the room they saw the three of us sitting around the fire laughing and decided we were to blame, but we feigned ignorance. Buddy had given them the SAAF version of a water bomb; a watermelon with a thunderflash implanted in it. Talk about ripping the ring out!

It was not long before he staggered off to the ablution block and started heaving up his guts. He was so bad that Brute hauled him off to the sickbay. The next morning Buddy was so *babalas* that they put him on a saline drip. In many ways he was lucky because VC was on the warpath.

We did a casevac first thing and, when we got back, I was summoned to VC's office. He sat behind his desk with a floor plan of the mess in front of him, with lines drawn across it that traced trajectories of the rolls and butter as reported by previous interviewees. It looked a bit like a spider's web at that stage and when he saw me, he knew I was innocent.

"Waars 'dai bosvark vriend van jou, ek kry hom nerens?" he growled, *"Ek gaan sy fokken nek afdraai."* (Where's that bushpig you call a friend; I'm going to wring his fucking neck). Buddy was safe in the sickbay for the time being

and hopefully would be well enough for the hammering VC had planned for him later. I got grilled, but I truly did not know what had happened and VC began to realize this was a futile exercise. In the end he asked who I thought had started it and again I could not help, but the chopper table would have been a safe bet.

As I left, I bumped into the Dominee outside and I told him what VC was up to. He had not been summoned, obviously because he was above suspicion, but then I remembered that he had been at the chopper table.

"I can sort this out very quickly." He walked into VC's office and took responsibility for the whole fiasco, and the drama of the whole incident simply fizzled out.

I spent the rest of the morning helping to clean up the mess and very impressive it was. I also noticed the unusual amount of uniforms hanging out to dry, so I guess a good time was had by all.

14
Angola Ops

"They are destroying my country"
Angolan President

One of the most effective ways of disrupting enemy activity is to destroy their supply lines. Looking at the geography of Angola, the two most obvious entry points for military ordnance would be by sea, through the capital Luanda and a smaller port further south called Mocamedes. From Luanda to the southern town of Ongiva, the fastest route would have been by rail to Xangongo on the Cunene river, over a very dilapidated bridge, and then finally by one of the few tarred roads in the region. The bridge had been bombed continuously since hostilities began and still stood, against all odds, albeit in a highly modified form. The railway from Luanda and the road from Mocamades both snaked through the mountains of the southern highlands and it was at this area that Brigadier Viljoen was pointing his cane. The fact that a Brig was in charge of this one gave us some idea of the importance of the op. Also, the targets were deep inside Angola, so thorough planning was essential and, because it was peak rain season, the weather had to be factored in as well.

"So, we have three targets: the bridge at Xangongo, the pass on the Mocamedes road here, and the railway tunnel here." The end of his cane tapped lightly on the three points deep inside Angola. "The temporary base will be set up here at Ruacana." I could see the blue line of the Cunene River travelling directly south, turning sharply west at the South West African and Angolan border. Ruacana had a hydro-electric dam and an airfield that had been turned into an Army camp to defend it. "And a forward base with the MAOT, fuel for the Pumas and a medical unit will be set up over here." He pointed to an area about fifty kilometres inside Angola, where there was absolutely nothing on the map, just savannah land. "The Pumas will operate in three groups of two choppers each. Group Alpha will leave from Ruacana and drop two sections of Recces north of Xangongo on the river, who will then use two inflatable boats to access the bridge and take it out." He pointed to a photo of the bridge that was well and truly buggered. It looked like pieces of five different bridges had been stuck together in a very *maak 'n plan* fashion and it was obvious that every trick in the book had been used to keep it operational. Well, it was about to get yet another pasting. "Group Bravo will take the railway tunnel here at Ponto Alta." That was Jim and me. I stared at the map. The tunnel was actually high up on the side of a mountain and there were no photos to get an idea of what we were looking for. "Group Charlie will take the road pass here." The road and railway line followed a similar path along the side of the range for a few kilometres from where we had to blow up the tunnel, but cut back sharply at one point and then snaked down a pass to the flatlands below. "The road is supported by a concrete bridge here and that is the target." He pointed to the spot with his finger, while squinting closely at the map. "We don't believe the tunnel and the bridge are guarded; they are simply too far inland and we have never hit them before, so everyone will be lightly armed to keep the weight down in the choppers, and obviously they have to carry the explosives and maximum fuel."

"Klausie, I want you to lead the formation to this river where Bravo and Charlie will split and proceed to their respective targets."

So Jim and I were group Bravo. We spent an hour gleaning every bit of information we could from the map. What worried us was the large expanse of flat grassland between Ruacana and the mountains. Flying low level at night, there was absolutely nothing to navigate on except maybe a few streams marked on the map. I knew from experience that there were no roads, only tracks that got washed over in the rainy season. The ops room also had nothing of any help, so they called headquarters at Oshakati to see if they had anything we could use. So it looked like it was going to be a heading and time exercise, which was pretty much what we were used to, as there was precious little to navigate on for many miles around Ondangwa. But it was going to be very difficult so far into Angola. A few degrees off over such a large distance and you would miss the target with very little chance of finding it. I spoke to the Brig about it and he looked genuinely worried.

The next day I was handed an envelope by one of the clerks and found a small map inside. It was neatly hand drawn, with no scale and coloured in with crayons, showing a number of rivers and a few points to look out for on the mountain range. It came from one of the Recce brass in Pretoria, who had heard about my concerns via the Brig. Crude as it was, it had a lot more useable detail than the topographic map issued by our government. Between the two maps, I thought we had a fighting chance of finding the tunnel and I spent some time with my co-pilot, Dave, planning the navigation.

Late that afternoon, the eight Pumas took off for Ruacana and we arrived just before sunset. We had a light supper and then the two Pumas that were going to set up the temporary refuelling base set off. We settled down to wait for our take off time at 21h00. As the evening wore on, the sky to the north started pulsing gently with white light and it was obvious we were going to have thunderstorms to deal with as well. The Puma crews gathered together and we went over the plan again. We had a chat about the weather and decided there would be no contingency plan. If there was a storm at the target area we would simply land and wait for it to pass; there would be no turning back for any reason, except major mechanical problems.

At 20h30 we made our way out to the choppers and did the pre-flight checks. We had full fuel tanks and an extra ferry tank as well, along with five hundred pounds of explosives, a demolition team of six; five Recces and an engineer who would supervise the positioning of the charges in the tunnel. If I had eaten too much supper the Puma would have been overweight, but we would have burned off a fair amount of fuel by the time we did the drop on the mountain, so I wasn't too worried about our weight at the target. I noticed the moon peeping through the rolling clouds above us and the wind picking up from the west, so there was also a good chance of a storm on the way to the mountain.

We started up and all six of us took off together and headed out west for ten kilometres, we then turned north and crossed over the Cunene River into Angola. Once over the river, there were a few rocky hills and then the flat savannah that worried me so much. There were no reference points to navigate on, as shown on the map, but there was a large river approximately halfway, on both the topographical map and the hand drawn one, that had a large kink in it. I was counting on this as a waypoint. After ten minutes, the two Alpha Pumas peeled away and headed to their drop off point north of Xangongo.

We flew on in the darkness at about a hundred feet, until we must have been close to the river and I asked Dave for a time check. As he lifted the map, the air rushing past his open window caught it and it disappeared into the night, literally ripped right out of his hands. "The fucking map's gone," he looked at me sheepishly, as Oogies our engineer howled with laughter. This was unbelievable. We were hundreds of kilometres into Angola in deteriorating weather, on our way to the trickiest job I had ever done, with quarter of a ton of dynamite on board and we had lost our primary source of navigation … … … All we had now was a neatly coloured-in sketch, probably done by someone's kid in 5 minutes flat! I checked our time; we must have flown over the river as well, so for all intents and purposes we were lost.

"Did you see the river?" I called Jim over the radio, breaking the radio silence.

"Negative."

So now we had no time reference either. I knew Abie, who was flying the lead chopper in Charlie, had only planned his navigation from our waypoint at the mountains and although it was only a few minutes away, finding that waypoint was going to be very difficult now. I decided to keep my mouth shut about the map and it was impossible to be cross with Dave. He had almost no bush experience and he was also the same rank as me, plus I had stroked the cat many times when I was a *sandsak.*

So we stuck to the heading and time and sure enough, after what seemed like ages, me sweating like a pig, the mountains loomed darkly ahead lit occasionally by lightning. As we got closer, I realized that even if we had had the map there was nothing to navigate on, so with the range about two kilometres away, I started climbing. I guessed that the wind direction would have changed as we got closer to the storm and I had offset my heading to compensate for the wind on the plains, so logically we should have been left off track. I banked slowly right and ended up parallel to the mountains and my heart sank even further. We needed a miracle to find the pass and tunnel in these conditions and for the first time I thought of cancelling the mission. Even if we had found the waypoint, our chances would have been marginal. Then, as has happened so often in my flying career, I had a stroke of luck. On the side of the mountain far ahead, I could just see a line of vehicle headlights snaking up the pass and I knew instantly that we had established Abie's target. I was very surprised how close to the waypoint we were, having drifted a few kilometres to the left, probably because I had over compensated for the wind. That on its own was a huge relief, but we still had a job to do. Why were there so many cars or trucks? Was it a convoy? I thought of warning Abie not to take on the perceived enemy presence, but he was a big boy and quite capable of making his own decisions.

Abie broke away from the formation behind us and made off to the pass. Now all we had to do was find our tunnel. I got a bit closer to the mountain and started to climb. As we went up, the turbulence became worse until we were bouncing around quite badly and I couldn't see a thing, except when the lightning flashed. I knew the tunnel was about two thirds of the way up, so I turned west and flew parallel to the range desperately looking for any hint of the railway line. Dave was squinting at the hand-drawn map using his penlight torch. I was beginning to wonder if he had lost the plot, when he pointed to a rounded peak on the range ahead of us and a sheer cliff to our right, both only visible in the lightning, saying the tunnel was midway between the two. Sure enough within a minute the lightning flashed and reflected on the railway line winding along the mountainside. I turned in closer and followed the line and as the rails disappeared, I knew we had found our target. I flicked down the landing gear lever and there was a flurry of activity in the back.

"Can you see me, Jim?"

"Negative." Even with the lightning, the camouflage of the Puma would make it invisible.

"I am going to orbit to the left and go in at ninety degrees to the mountain, position behind me." I switched on the nav lights for a few seconds for Jim's benefit, and heard the doors slide open behind me.

As we levelled off after the orbit, it started raining. The tunnel mouth was ahead and the single-track railway line was very close to the side of the mountain. I could see even from this distance that there was no place to land. As we got closer it started to hammer down and I couldn't see a thing, so I brought the chopper into the hover, maybe fifty feet from the cliff and told Oogies to talk me in. This was it. I was going to land and there was no way I was going to chicken out. We were being thrown around by the wind and I was almost at full power trying to keep it steady enough to land. Yet to make matters worse, the landing light was reflecting off the rain producing nothing but a bright glare in front of me. My only reference was through my side window and I could just make out the railway. I inched forward as Oogies, hanging out of the side door, talked me in and soon the edge of the cliff and the railway appeared underneath. I placed the nose wheel of the Puma between the lines as gently as I could.

"Don't move forward!" Oogies cautioned. Effectively we were still flying because the main landing gear and the tail of the chopper were hanging over the cliff edge, and I was concentrating so much on the landing that when I looked up, I got a big shock. The main rotor was only a few feet away from the cliff in front of me. If I had touched the rock face with the rotor blades we would have been toast.

The Recces started throwing their equipment onto the ledge and jumped out as I lifted off and reversed back before turning and starting another orbit. Now it was Jim's turn. I warned him about the lack of space and he said he had been watching us. The Puma handled the turbulence much better with all the weight out of it, so I circled slowly as Jim did his drop without any drama.

We swooped down to the bottom of the mountain just as the rain stopped and found a level spot next to a small dry stream to land on. I didn't notice any dwellings in the area so I guessed we were going to have a quiet wait while the Recces did their business, a few thousand feet above us. They said they needed about an hour, but would call me on a small hand held walkie-talkie when they were finished. I switched on the walkie-talkie and stuck it in my pocket.

On the ground it was ominously quiet. Only the thunder rolled quietly in the distance, and the air was clean, fresh and still after the storm. I called everyone together and we decided on our respective lookout points surrounding the two Pumas. Oogies and I walked about a hundred metres down to the edge of the dry riverbed and lay down under a bush. We could see very little in the near pitch darkness, but the light-coloured river sand would contrast with anything moving along or crossing it. I was hoping the clouds would let a bit of moonlight through, but this was a double-edged sword, because it would also show up the silhouette of the Pumas.

We lay there in silence and my mind started wandering. We had been damn lucky but it occurred to me that the map would have been useless without light anyway. Dave would have to keep a tight grip on his maps in future. The look on his face was priceless.

The clouds were beginning to break and patches of moonlight illuminated the riverbed and surrounding bush. Something moved a short way up the river and my heart began to race. I stared intensely, but the moon disappeared and pitch darkness blanketed the bush again. I could hear footsteps moving quickly in the soft sand towards us, stopping every now and then, definitely human and quite agile, until they were very close and then suddenly they stopped right in front of me. Every one of my senses was screaming. My R4 was pointed straight at whoever it was and I felt my thumb on the safety switch and my forefinger on the trigger, but I couldn't see a thing. I could smell stale smoke and body odour laced with fear, and I wondered briefly if he could smell me. We faced each other for what seemed like ages and then the moon glowed through the clouds and my hands tightened on the rifle. Before me stood a boy, maybe ten years old, and I realized he wasn't staring at me, but over my head at the Pumas on the raised ground behind us.

"Nick, come in. We are ready for the pick up." The radio crackled in my pocket. I jumped clean off the ground with fright and the boy shot back up the riverbed at full sprint. Oogies grunted, just as surprised as I was. If I had released the safety on my R4 that youngster would be dead … … . I still get the heebies thinking about that incident.

I was drenched in sweat and shaking like a leaf as we made our way back to the choppers, with Oogies asking me if I was okay. I suppose he had many more years experience than me and the pressure didn't bother him as much. Some guys got tougher as the years passed and some started falling to bits, but none stayed the same.

We started up and did a long climbing turn up to the tunnel. This time we got a few flashes from a torch to show us where to land. The pickup, compared to the drop off, was a piece of cake. We both landed on the railway at the same time and I rested the nose wheel on the outside rail, using it to stabilize us in the hover, plus we were a lot lighter without all the dynamite, our fuel was going down and there was much less turbulence. The engineer fiddled with a small box at the entrance to the tunnel and then got into Jim's chopper smartly. We backed away from the cliff and headed south towards home, and I was pleased to see we had enough fuel to go directly back to Ruacana, without stopping at the temporary forward base. All in all I was quite happy with how things had panned out, shaky as they were, and the operation showed all the signs of a success.

We had been airborne about five minutes when there was a big yellow flash behind us, distinctly different from the lightning, and the Recces cheered in the back. Mission accomplished.

Back at Ruacana there were sandwiches and beers waiting for us. Abie landed about ten minutes after us, his op a success too. They had landed on the road and set up a roadblock while they laid the charges, much to the bewildered amazement of the civilians using the pass. The road was very busy because it was a public holiday and this was the way back from the coast to the inland towns. They must have been mightily pissed-off when their road home disappeared in a cloud of smoke and tumbled down the side of the mountain.

Alpha had to abort their op because there was too much activity in the town and they stood no chance of blowing the bridge without being spotted. We considered Xangongo to be a military installation and engaging the enemy with such a small force would have been crazy, so they were picked up minus their rubber ducks which they slashed and burned next to the river.

The next day the Angolan President complained to the United Nations that we were destroying his country. I wondered what exactly he had expected to happen in a war.

That little hand-drawn map is stuck away somewhere. I think the person who drew it would be very surprised at how important it turned out to be.

15
Squadron Life

"So, what's it like being a pilot?"
"Great ... beats working for a living."

Back at Ondangwa there was nothing to do but read and lay in the sun by our little duckpond swimming pool, while we waited for the Flossie to take us home the next day. From the rest area we could hear the constant movement of aircraft in and out – it was a busy war, low intensity or otherwise. Impalas taking off two by two, Pumas, Alouettes and the drone of piston-engined aircraft such as Kudus, Bosboks, Cessnas and the ubiquitous Dakota. Occasionally a Flossie bringing supplies and fresh personnel or a Citation with visiting brass broke the pattern. There was also a constant stream of pilots and engineers in and out and you could easily speak to a hundred people in one day, gleaning snippets of information from each one of them.

"Diggers had a bike prang ... he's OK, just a couple of roasties ... taxi *klapped* him at Fountains Circle. Bikes fucked."

"Mike and Sherry have broken up. She says he drinks too much."

" ... found a bomb at Alberton Mall ... didn't go off ... "

"PW's coming to visit next week ... "

" ... heard rumours of a big op coming up ... "

"Baasie flew into telephone lines near Potch ... always ripping the ring out."

Then Oogies appeared. "Puma 166 must to go back for a major (service), but they want it at Atlas tomorrow. If we leave now we can be home before midnight." That was enough for Jiggs and me. We gathered our kit, signed for the aircraft at the ops room and arrived just as Oogies was finishing the fuelling. Within half an hour we were thundering down the road to Grootfontein and Jim started a slow climb up to ten thousand feet. Flying at altitude was quite safe outside the red zone simply because nobody lived more than ten minutes south of Ondangwa. The area was quite barren, with even the hardy thorn bushes thinly spread amongst the vast expanses of sterile salt pans.

Soon a massive white patch appeared on the land in front of us. It spread as far as we could see – the Etosha Pan. The Etosha Pan is one of a number of unique natural features in this part of Africa, so big it looks like an inland sea in the summer as the breeze ripples the water and shimmers in the sunlight, yet it is only a foot or so deep. Literally millions, if not billions of birds breed and rear their young here before departing north for the winter, and every description of game arrives for a feast that lasts for months. Far below us the uniform milky surface was broken by patches of different colours as the colonies of birds celebrated the facets of procreation.

Past the pan the bush was a uniform emerald green; a combination of grass and thorn bush with the fence lines of very large cattle farms and outcrops of granite *koppies* breaking the monotony. Someone told me, probably a Namibian farmer, that the best beef in the world came from there because the grass and thorn bush leaves were sweet. I must say the meat we got for our *braais* at Ondangwa was as good as any I can remember.

We landed at Windhoek and refuelled quickly. The countryside between Windhoek and Upington was an absolute zero for me; just hundreds of miles of red sand dunes with no signs of life, and from five hundred feet and forty degrees centigrade seemed sterile and dearth, forgotten and largely unexplored by man and beast. As I write these words I can sense outraged naturalists baying at my ignorance because it does support a wonderfully unique and diverse wildlife, its remoteness a saving grace against the relentless goose-step of materialist man. While exercising extreme care not to wander too far from our flight plan in case we ended up on this parched Mars-scape, it was possible to fly along a dry riverbed most of the way, but even this got boring after a while. The riverbed was so dry that farmers had built their houses and outbuildings on it, a tricky decision given that the bed was thirty to fifty feet deep, and at least a hundred wide, which left one pondering the volume of water that scoured a feature of that magnitude out of the desert. Indeed, every fifty years or so the puzzling remains of some farms litter the beaches of the Skeleton Coast to the west, debris resulting from powerful flash floods that have annihilated everything in their path and spewed the whole lot into the sea.

We had a good laugh when we flew over one farm holding, quite literally in the middle of nowhere, and I looked it up on the map. It was called "Lithgow." There are some crazy Scotsmen on this planet, but what the hell were my kinsfolk doing there!?

As we crossed the border of South West Africa and South Africa it was quite obvious that the level of human activity increased dramatically. The Richtersvelt is as close to a moonscape as imaginable and appeared unoccupied, but there were a number of wind pumps next to reservoirs full to the brim with water and some very fat and happy cattle roaming around, these giving clues to prosperous farms and a more dynamic culture. Upington was more interesting with its wine farms built on islands in the Orange River and as we detoured over the Augrabies Falls, an impressive show of power was proved as the summer rains crashed into the gorge.

It was getting late and the sun would set in an hour, so again we hurried the refuelling and I flew the last leg as night set in. The towns we passed were patches of lights becoming more frequent as we progressed … Klerksdorp, Parys, Potchefstroom, and then the ADF needle for Swartkops steadied as we approached the vast carpet of lights called the Witwatersrand. Egoli, Big Smoke, Joeys, P-Town … but ultimately it was civilization! And soon we were landing just before midnight, still wide awake and full of energy, second guessing which pubs might be open. But after Oogies had towed the Puma into the 19 Squadron hangar, a Corolla saloon arrived and a very polite young officer took us to SAAFCOL for a snack and a good night's sleep.

❖❖

The next morning we arrived at 19 Squadron to be told that 166 was to go to Atlas immediately and that there was a Puma ready to go back to Durban waiting for us there. Splendid news, which meant we would be home for lunch. Jim immediately phoned Sandy and organized a lunch at the Father's Moustache pub and hopefully Van could get some time off as well.

At Atlas we waited half an hour while the techs fiddled with one of the radios and then we set sail over the cattle and *mielie* fields of the Highveld, until we got to the escarpment near Van Reenen. Here the whole feel of the country changed as we flew into a vast basin of flawless clarity. This was our turf. To the south towered the majestic Drakensburg, to the north lay rolling green hills rich with forests and farms. In front was the sea – over two hundred kilometres away on a day of abnormal visibility. In the space of twenty four hours we had transversed Southern Africa from one corner to the other in my favourite means of transport, and I was mightily impressed. What an amazing and beautiful country!

We landed in good time and presented ourselves to our commanding officer to whom we gave a debrief of the operation and caught up with the local goings-on and gossip. Word of the pub lunch had got around and everyone except the standby crew was going to be there, plus a few guys from 5 Squadron who shared the base with us.So, without ado, we went back to our flat on the Bluff for a shower and to put on our jeans and *takkies*.

❖❖

Father's was full and although we were all dressed in civvies it was quite obvious that most of the people were from the various military institutions around Durban. I recognised a few Recces, always game for a party, looking quite strange not up to their eyes in filth and smeared with camo make-up, and some of the local Navy divers. There was also plenty of National Servicemen there.

The air was thick with smoke, the smell of beer and as usual the aircon was set too cold, but the mood was festive. Van and Sandy were already seated in a corner and cheered when they saw us, showering us with hugs and kisses. They both looked gorgeous. Ah, it was good to be home!

We had a hamburger, a few beers and watched quite awestruck as Sandy won the ladies down-down competition – by a very comfortable margin I might add, impressing all the the blokes and shocking all the girls that such a lovely young woman was actually an A-Team tomboy. Jiggs was so stoked his eyes were brimming with tears and it was obvious these two were destined to make a good partnership.

That night we had supper at Stax, our favourite steak house on Marine Parade, and on Saturday Van was working, so I spent the day reading and gave my bike a good polish.

Sundays were always very active; I picked Van up early on my bike and we went on the breakfast run up to Hilton with Jim, Steel and Roy. Unlike in Johannesburg where everyone did their own thing, we all gathered on West Street near the Beach Hotel and rode together in a group of over a hundred bikes. If someone had a problem, it was not unusual for the whole lot of us to stop and wait. There were also a large number of XT500 scramblers that rode with us, a very popular bike in Durban, which could not keep up with the super bikes so we all rode at a more sedate pace. When we had breakfast everyone was friends and there were no social barriers, it was really most enjoyable and a highlight of the week. Afterwards the four bikes from our squadron set off for Ballito to visit Glen, the lifesaver who had become a friend of the SAAF. Thereafter, we would meet Andy at Hazelmere Dam for some sailing on his Hobie Cat and enjoy a *braai* in the afternoon. In the evening we usually went to the Mykonos Restaurant in West Street and finished off the weekend with a really good meal.

❖❖

The next morning when we got to work there were two Pumas on the hardstand so it was a safe bet that something was cooking. We sat down for a briefing with some senior policemen from Durban and listened to a situation report about faction fighting in the Valley of a Thousand Hills, not even ten minutes flying from the base. Apparently there had been an attempted rape among the local population and the perpetrator had been murdered. The whole episode had spiralled out of control to the point where a few hundred men had taken sides and the casualties were mounting at an alarming rate. The police were moving into the area and the two Pumas would be there to back them up. Steel and I would be in one aircraft and Jim and Roy in the other, both of us operating independently under the guidance of two police liaison officers who we would carry with us. We set off and spent the first hour positioning groups for roadblocks. The area was swarming with police and the exercise was very well co-ordinated. By lunchtime we had a pile of weapons the size of a small house, from traditional spears and knives to homemade guns, some of which were crudely fashioned from household pipes and conduit and using a washing peg to fire with. It's a fair assumption that many of the casualties were caused by these makeshift weapons exploding in their operator's hands. There were also a huge number of proper guns such as hunting rifles and shotguns, some of which looked very expensive and many with their barrels sawn in half, as well as a lot of handguns. Most of which had been stolen in burglaries and robberies all over Natal. Our liaison officer said a number of stolen police weapons had been recovered, many of which were taken from injured policemen doing riot control or from officers attacked in the townships during the course of their duties.

Literally hundreds of men, many of them bearing ugly cuts and gashes from the fighting, were loaded into trucks and carted off to Durban for fingerprinting and processing, with a number of wanted criminals netted in the process. It was hard to believe that such savagery existed in those rolling green hills.

The next day was quiet so I put my name down for a general flying period. We were allowed to fly a certain number of hours a month that was classified as training and to keep our skills honed. Most often we practiced emergencies and simulated power off landings or did some simulated instrument flying. On rare occasions we did what we called a "jolly", a flight that had no formal structure or significance, perhaps taking National Servicemen on a flip around Durban or along the coast and this is what I had planned to do.

Jim, Botter and I set off through the gap in the Bluff and flew along the beach to Amanzimtoti and then onto the Umkomaas River lagoon. From there it was low flying up the river valley that wound its way almost to Pietermaritzburg. There were no power or telephone lines crossing the river on the way so you could really crank it and follow the river with the valley towering on either side. Co-ordination, judgement and speed control had to be spot on as every bend was different, plus you could not see what was coming up next. Furthermore, the Puma was quite heavy even when empty so you also had to compensate for the inertia.

From Maritzburg we flew over Kersney College where Jim had a cousin at school, just to say "howzit," and then to Salt Rock and back along the coast to Virginia Airport, where we requested a runway inspection. This involved flying flat out along the runway at ten feet and doing a wing over at the end. Pure showmanship for the civvies, but great fun nonetheless, and then over the harbour and back to the airport. This whole round trip had taken just under an hour, so we did some simulated power off landings and emergencies on the runway to make up the hour.

Just before home time we were told the first standby crew, which was Steel, Duppie and I, had to stay on at the base in anticipation of a mountain rescue because a couple had been reported missing in the Drakensberg. A mountain rescue team was getting close to them but conditions were deteriorating and they felt it would be better to airlift them out. We decided to fly to Winterton and land at the police station while the mountaineers sorted themselves out, as it would cut at least an hour off of the rescue time.

We took off a short while later and even from Durban we could see the clouds over the Berg, which meant three things: wind, possibly rain, and that it would be dark when we did the pickup. One consolation was that we had one of the most spectacular sunsets I have ever seen. The horizon was black contrasting with a deep maroon and spread through the entire glorious spectrum to indigo above us. The shape of the clouds were accentuated with pink and orange but, however magnificent the scenery was, it spelt bad news for us.

When we got to Winterton it was already dark and the police told us a doctor and two mountaineers were waiting at the Drakensburg Gardens Hotel. They would be our guides to the pickup and fly back with the two climbers to King Edwards Hospital in Durban. We did not shut down and, as it turned out, leaving early was a good decision, so we took off immediately. The drop in temperature was quite dramatic and we got bumped around a fair bit in the turbulence, but luckily there was no rain. We could see the hotels and farms spread over the area as patches of light on a pitch dark background. There was no definition to the mountains, but we would tackle that problem in due course.

Using the patches of lights on the ground, I cross-referenced the hotel on my map and we found it without any trouble. We landed on the hotel airstrip and shut the aircraft down so that we could brief and get our heads around this rescue, which was looking trickier by the minute. There was a bit of moonlight peeping through the clouds to the east, but the heavy clouds gathering above us were occasionally illuminated with flashes of lightning, still far away but definitely cause for concern, and the wind was picking up. The couple were quite close to the hotel, only a few kilometres away as the crow flies, but the husband had injured his hip in a fall and his wife was fine apart from being cold and in shock.

I worked out the navigation while Duppie checked the hoist and Steel gleaned as much information from the rescue team as possible. The rescue would be from the bank of a stream that had a vertical cliff and trees next to it, but the other side of the stream sloped upwards with no trees and seemed a much better pick up point. The problem was that the stream was flowing strongly and the mountaineers were not able to cross it with a stretcher.

We started up and set off over the two hills and valleys to the north of the hotel, descending into the third valley flying really slowly at about forty knots and twenty feet above the stream, with our landing light illuminating the terrain in front. The wind was on the nose, one of the few things in our favour, but we were getting bumped around by the turbulence. I asked Steel if he wanted the undercarriage up or down and he said 'up' as it would not have made much difference if we ended up in the stream, which was full of boulders anyway! After a few minutes the valley narrowed and we had to climb to sixty feet before it opened up to reveal a cliff rising vertically to the right and in front of us, with the sloping ground rising to our left. This was where the valley ended, with directly in front of us was a waterfall that I had not picked up on the map. It seemed to start raining, but we soon realised that our rotor wash was blowing water from the waterfall all over the place and it was settling on the windscreen, reflecting in the landing light. Occasionally the rock faces glowed briefly like ghosts peering down at us as the lightning penetrated the clouds above and gave us the only clue as to our surroundings. This was turning out to be one hell of a pickup.

We saw the torches of the rescuers flickering next to the stream so Steel fixed the landing light on some rocks to his right and settled into a very bumpy hover, with Duppie lowering the hoist cable to the ground. It was a about fifty feet and we couldn't get any closer because of the trees, so it seemed to take for ages, but a few minutes later the hoist arrived back with the woman who was bundled into the back of the aircraft and covered in blankets by the doctor.

Steel was working really hard keeping the chopper steady, but there were no complaints from Duppie whose job it was to conduct the lift. He would be exhausted in five minutes with this workload and I got ready to take over if he wanted a rest. The rescue team seemed to take an abnormally long time, but they had to attach a stretcher this time and I almost gasped with relief when I heard the hoist whining as it lifted the husband to safety. Duppie and the doctor pulled him aboard and we were finished.

As Steel moved slowly away from the cliff he turned the nose toward the sloping ground. We started bumping around quite badly and then suddenly the landing light went out and everything went black. I sensed the chopper accelerating as the wind pushed us from behind and Steel desperately tried to get the nose up, but we were already at full power. A flash of lightning gave us an instant to orientate and Steel whipped the tail around and got the nose pointing down the stream-bed. The chopper accelerated very quickly now as we flew over the narrow section and it seemed as if the hand of God was pushing us down as we hit a massive downdraught, and the Puma sank like a stone. Steel hit the contingency power button but there was nothing left as we shuddered and bounced in the turbulence. Within a second the water washing over the boulders was dimly visible a few feet below us as we screamed down the valley almost out of control. Then another flash of lightning and that was all Steel needed to get his bearings, lifting us into a climb and clear of the valley. I glanced into the back to see everyone lying flat on the floor – they obviously thought we were tickets, but we made it!

I flew the leg back to the hospital and, on the way, Duppie stuck his head into the cockpit and asked if we had hit anything. I thought there had been a bump, but Steel was not sure. We had just been through a heck of ordeal and put it down to the excitement, but the flight controls felt quite normal to me.

Back at the base Duppie towed the Puma into the hangar and we discovered what a close shave it had been. One of the HF aerials underneath the belly was torn from its mountings and the remains of the aerial wire were wrapped around the tail rotor hub. I pointed out that Steel had decided to keep the undercarriage retracted and, but for that, the landing gear would have hit the rocks and, at the very least, the aircraft would have been severely damaged. Considering the gear forms part of the hydraulic system, we may well have pranged altogether. The landing light had simply burned out, admittedly at the worst possible time. It's a very powerful light and it needs airflow over it to keep it cool and there were limitations on how long it could be used in the hover.

Steel was a year or so ahead of me and I had been his co-pilot for many hours during my *sandsak* days. I had a lot of confidence in his ability and that night was one of the finest displays of airmanship I can remember. He had the instincts and co-ordination of a cat, plus guts and an incredibly cool head under pressure.

❖❖

It was good to be back at the squadron and civvy street for a reasonable length of time as we were spending a hell of a lot of time in the bush. I had been on the squadron about a year when I sat down one day and worked out that we spent four out of six weeks on the border and we were flying an average of eighty hours a month, which was close to the maximum time a pilot was allowed to fly by law. But the laws were created largely with airline pilots in mind, who spent most of their airborne time monitoring the aircraft systems. Compared to them our flying was very busy, with a wide variety of operational requirements and lots of flying at low level, without the luxury of auto pilots and sophisticated navigation systems. Plus, the chance of getting shot at was always there and we had to deal with increasing frequencies of mechanical emergencies, as the wear and tear on the choppers was starting to take effect.

My love life was suffering as well. Van was an amazing girlfriend, but to expect her to hang in there while I spent so much time away was simply unfair and I'm sure it crossed her mind that at some stage I might not come back at all. We had a strangely detached sort of relationship and I was never exactly sure where I stood. I was too scared to ask her in case she told me the truth.

I knew I wanted to spend less time in the bush, so I was considering doing an instructors course or moving onto another aircraft, such as the Dak, that would allow me to spend more time at home. But irrespective of that, I would have to leave Durban and I was not sure if Van would come with me.

I think the other guys had similar problems. Jim and Sandy struck me as being a perfect couple. Van and Sandy always hung out together when we were away and although Van never said anything, I got the impression she was ready to get married. So while we were all together for a brief period we decided to go away for a weekend in the Drakensberg. In order to save a few bob, Van made the booking through her contacts in the hotel industry, and we set off to the Eagle's Nest Hotel one Saturday morning in Jim's little Alphasud.

The hotel was built in a crag at the foot of Cathedral Peak that towered majestically overhead, with a runway built on the only piece of flat ground for miles around and a couple of small dams lined with ancient trees that led up to the old stone buildings. The scenery was impossibly beautiful and it was spring, so the fresh green leaves and the scents freed by the first showers, gave the atmosphere a mystic freshness that was intoxicating.

At reception, we booked a hike and a pony ride and then made our way to our cottage, built of stone with a beamed thatch roof and a large fireplace facing a soft down bed.

We had a light lunch and set off on the hike, following a path that crossed a crystal clear stream and wound its way up and over a series of small rocky hills. The top of each hill revealed one breathtaking view after another, as the sheer black cliffs swept upwards for thousands of feet contrasting sharply with the silver blue sky and, on the other side, the green hills rolled on forever. Our guide pointed out landmarks and points of historical interest when we stopped on the crests, panting from exertion, but his words went largely unheard, as the experience of this beauty was simply overwhelming. This place was sacred.

Hiking was altogether more fulfilling than flying around there in a chopper, which in a way was a travesty because of the noise and the lack of effort we made in accessing those beautiful places.

Without realizing it we had walked around in a large circle and after a few hours the hotel appeared in front of us like an oasis. The sun had passed over the mountain and it was getting dark and very cold, so we decided to have a shower first and then meet in the pub for a few drinks before supper. As we walked into the cottage the flames from the fireplace danced gently on the walls, and the thatch ceiling absorbed all sound except the crackling of the logs.

It was as if I had moved through an ethereal membrane into a different world, and the choppers and the war were the furthest things from my mind.

I'd always felt a bit shy when Van and I were alone together, the price you pay when you spend so little time together that intimate boundaries are hardly explored or established, so I let her bathe alone, while I had a beer on the veranda and watched the last light of a perfect day melt into the heavens. When she emerged, she was absolutely glowing, with rosy cheeks and clear blue eyes and I was a little shocked to realize how pretty she was. We had been going out for just less than a year and I suddenly realized I hardly knew her.

We made our way up to the pub, which was packed, mostly with young couples on a weekend away like us. The hi-fi banged out rock music that was strangely out of place in the rustic setting, but the atmosphere was vibrant. We had a few drinks followed by supper. Jim and Sandy decided to go to the disco, but I was totally bushed and suggested to Vanessa that we have a quiet glass of wine in the room in front of the fire.

Back in the room, I threw a few more logs on the fire and Van pulled the huge duvet off the bed onto the floor. I poured us a glass of wine each and we stared at each other in silence, like fascinated strangers, as the flames danced in her eyes and the corners of her lips invited me with a delicate smile. We kissed, letting the desire melt into passion, and slowly undoing all the knots that had held us apart for so long. She was so soft and smelled like stream water bubbling over pebbles, letting my mouth play with her as my passion turned to delicious agony, and I couldn't wait any longer. She was perfect. Finally the waves of ecstasy washed over us until, finally, we collapsed in exquisite exhaustion.

This was different. For the first time I wanted Van close to me. Other instincts were being aroused that I was unfamiliar with – mysterious, deliciously tempting and thought provoking – deeply so. I was in love. How I was going to dovetail this into my career didn't occur to me at that stage.

❖❖

A string of bad experiences has made me very wary of horses, so I was not really looking forward to the pony ride. However, the next morning we all trooped down to the stables and stood around chatting as the horses were saddled. The groom allocated each of us a horse and I found myself mounted on a large gelding, which I was told is a stallion without balls. My suspicion should have been aroused by the way the groom presented this information; wide-eyed, toothless and standing well clear. But these animals seemed well worn and were no doubt used to dealing with all sorts of incompetence, so to my mind there was nothing to worry about.

We moved off down to the river at a leisurely pace but my horse lagged well behind and frustratingly didn't respond to any of my commands. This was the second warning signal, but I put it down to a total lack of horsemanship on my part. What was extremely annoying and uncomfortable was the way he moved. Each step the horse took was out of sync with the upward and downward momentum of my body, so my backside banged down on the saddle with every step. Every effort to make the horse move a bit faster to break this rhythm was ignored. After a mere ten minutes, I had had enough. My arse was so sore that I found myself alternately standing and gripping the saddle with my knees, which had its own set of discomforts, and then sitting and shuffling my backside around on the saddle trying to find some un-pulverized flesh. On and on it went. Oblivious to my misery, everyone else was thoroughly enjoying the ride through the magnificent scenery, so I decided not to spoil the fun by complaining.

We made our way across the grass runway around a steep embankment, onto the road and then onto a pathway next to the dams. The path was narrow, meandering between the dams and a line of oak trees. Mercifully the slower single file pace forced my steed to stop his shit and I was able to chat with the others and admire the glass-like surface of the dams, along with the snow-capped mountains towering above us. Eventually, the path ended at the top of a dam wall, where we stood around for a while before the groom turned his horse and we started back to the hotel.

On turning around my nag showed an uncharacteristic amount of energy. He barged, rather rudely I thought, past the other horses scraping my ankle painfully on the stirrup of Jim's horse in the process! It crossed my mind to drive the bloody thing into the dam and get finished. But that deliciously mischievous thought lasted only a moment.

He bolted forward so quickly that were it not for the reins I would have somersaulted backwards onto the ground. When I sat upright there was a split second before my head smacked a low oak tree branch and the little helmet flew off my head as I was knocked back again, but this time my feet came up and I was totally out of control. I bounced in the saddle a few times and miraculously stayed on, only to be thrown forward as he hesitated before leaping over a ditch. I stayed low and managed to grab onto his mane as the other low branches, which I hadn't noticed on the way in, flashed past inches above my head.

He galloped down the narrow path until we had to turn onto the road, and despite his size, swept deftly around the corner and onto the road. My initial shock was over and I realized with relief that apart from the car park and a long driveway, we would be back at the stables in a few minutes. We galloped down the road and I could see the entrance in the distance, but when we got to the runway he veered suddenly towards the embankment and I sensed serious trouble. We careened over the edge and I braced myself for the impact, but he leapt over the terraces two at a time and landed at the bottom with a huge grunt, before stumbling briefly and starting to buck. I knew it was time for me to abandon ship, but as we bucked I felt my left foot slip forward in the stirrup … … I had the presence of mind to realize that jumping would get me trampled, so I hung on as we bounced around rodeo style for a while. Then he shook his head furiously realizing that his rider was stuck like a leech and took off straight down the runway at full stretch. We went so fast my eyes filled up with tears. All I could see was a blur, and in that blur could just be made out another tree at the end of the runway to which he was heading straight toward. It was obvious by now he used the trees to remove clumsy parasites like me from his back, but my life now depended on staying put. I had my arms around his neck, my knees clamped on the saddle and my loathing had turned to frozen terror. I was worried he was heading for the hills where he could do me in good and proper; that I would be found face down in a mountain stream by a rescue team with twisted HF antennae, and other hastily abandoned military paraphernalia. As the tree came closer I could see we were going to hit it. He slammed the tree hard with his shoulder and ricocheted off at an angle, stumbling sickeningly. I sensed another chance to jump off, but he caught his balance with cat-like agility and we clattered up the long stone pathway to the stables, where he screeched to a halt so quickly, that I slipped forward and fell head first into a pile of stable sweepings.

I jumped up and moved well away from him and we stood there staring at each other for a minute. We were both breathing very heavily with the whites of our eyes showing. As furious as he was, I sensed he was as amazed as me that I had made it so far.

The others arrived shortly after with everyone laughing and congratulating me on my horsemanship. But the big surprise was Van. She threw her arms around me and gave me a big smoochy kiss, horse shit and all, her eyes were positively sparkling with adoration. I knew then that this was my girl.

Back in Durban that evening, we were having a glass of wine and she mentioned coyly that we had been going out almost a year and began asking questions about my plans for the future. Although I enjoyed the SAAF, flying and the bush, I was simply spending too much time away from home. There was now a fork in my life which would involve losing my beloved Puma and this was deeply unsettling. Maybe I would opt for an instructor's course and study for my commercial pilot's licence, I really wasn't sure, but changes had to be made.

I decided to ask Van to marry me. I would keep it a surprise, go and get a ring the next morning and take her out for supper on Monday night. But I had to go back to the mess, so reluctantly we parted, yet I was so excited that I wanted to bust.

16

Mauritius 2

"Samaritan with teeth"
Herman Potgieter

The next morning there was a knock on our flat door at around sunrise. It was a guard from the base who told us to get to the squadron as soon as possible for an emergency. Jim and I were not on standby, so it was obviously a big problem needing a number of choppers. We pulled on jeans and T-shirts and shot off to the base at high speed in the pouring rain.

At the base four Pumas were on the hardstand with the ground crews swarming all over them and two fuel bowzers filling them up with AVTUR. The briefing room was packed. Four chopper crews and a group of Navy divers and medics sat around chatting noisily and smoking. As soon as we were all sat down, Major Foote started.

"There's a ship sinking, approximately eighty miles east-north-east and nineteen crew on board. The last call from the ship was about ten minutes ago, so we presume the crew is in the life rafts already, but it's not certain if the ship itself has sunk yet. Now it's a washing machine out there with a four metre swell and wind from the north-east at about twenty knots. Hoisting the sailors in these conditions is bloody dangerous and it's quite likely that there will be injuries, so each chopper will have a diver and two medics. The crew are all to be taken straight to Addington Hospital. These guys are Turkish so don't bring anyone back here to the base, because they will be handed over to the military police and it will just make life complicated. The police and the foreign affairs people will handle them at Addington."

The chopper crews got together to discuss a strategy. We paired up, with Peanuts and Jannie commanding the first two choppers, and Jim and myself in the second two. Jim and I would go out first and locate the ship and Peanuts and Jannie would follow depending on our fuel state and the way the rescue progressed. If we all went together, there was the danger that all four Pumas would run out of fuel looking for the lifeboats and we would have to leave people out there which, in turn, could lead to disaster. We made our way out to the dispersal area and did the pre-flights. Soon our two Pumas were powering over the airfield and out to sea.

The weather was atrocious. The cloud base was dark and patchy with the lowest at about three hundred feet, rain density changing constantly and the sea a churning mass of surf. The colour of both the sea and sky was a deep silvery grey and they blended perfectly so there was no horizon. This made judging height impossible so we had to fly on the radio altimeter at about two hundred feet, making the field of vision so small we would only see the ship when we were very close to it … presuming of course that it was still afloat. Furthermore, the FM direction finder was giving a very weak signal so if the ship had sunk, finding the lifeboats could be the next problem. We split up so that Jim was flying in line with me about a kilometre to my starboard as we flew further and further out, occasionally going through squalls of rain so heavy that we were flying blind. I found myself automatically scanning the instruments. We could quite easily have flown right over the ship and not seen it in those conditions.

After half an hour my adrenalin began to pump. This was crunch time; we had to find the ship within the next ten minutes or it would be obvious that something was wrong with our calculations. We would then have to start a grid search which would be close to meaningless in such conditions. I told Willie our engineer to open the doors and get the diver and medics to start scanning. Another ten minutes went by and still there was nothing. My heart began to sink. Jim radioed that he was beginning his grid search and I decided to fly on for another five minutes before I started mine. Those five minutes seemed like hours, and still nothing. We had been called out a few weeks before to look for a stricken fishing boat and the whole thing turned out to be bullshit. It was inconceivable that something as serious as this was a hoax. Or was it?

Then in the distance I saw a very unusual sight. A shaft of sunlight was beaming through the clouds like a searchlight. There was simply no other sunlight anywhere else, and where it met the sea I could faintly make out the shape of a ship lying on its side. I adjusted my heading slightly to port and called Jim, and sure enough within a few seconds the shaft of light was gone. I glanced at Andy my co-pilot to see if he had picked it up as well, but he was staring blankly into the grey gloom so I kept quiet. We had found the ship, hocus pocus or not, that was all that mattered.

As we got closer there was no doubt, even to my inexperienced eye, that the ship was going to sink. It was listing heavily to starboard and the deck was exposed to the relentless onslaught of the swell and wind. It looked as if the deck was packed with large rolls of cable that had broken loose and shifted onto the right hand side of the deck, which had in turn made the ship roll onto its side. The foul weather made sure there was no chance of redemption. I noted with interest that the ship looked new, only on its second voyage as I found out later, with Mauritius 2 emblazoned on the stern and bow in fresh white paint.

The lifeboats were missing which meant the crew was off the ship. Jim called that he had found one and as I turned west, I could see the orange hull of a lifeboat floating upside down in the churning sea just a short distance away. My heart sank. There was no sign of any bodies. We moved away from the ship in a large circle until, about two kilometres away, two more small orange hulls came into view, this time floating upright, the sailors waving frantically at us.

A short orbit around them and it was obvious that hoisting them up was going to be very difficult and dangerous. The only way to get them into the chopper would be to get them to jump into the sea, one by one, and then hoist them out of the water. Hoisting them out of the lifeboat would result in broken bones because it was pitching around in the swell so badly. After briefing Willie what to do, we lowered the diver into the water and waved for one of them to jump into the sea. I listened to Willie talking me over the target for a few minutes, but all I got was a very confusing set of instructions and it was clear we were getting nowhere. I couldn't see what was going on below us, which made it even more frustrating and eventually I lost my rag, demanding some decisive action.

The main problem was that it was impossible for me to judge my height above water and there was no reference to use for hovering, so the communication between Willie and me was critical. The swell was moving into the wind, carrying the diver with it, yet the wind was blowing the lifeboat away from the chopper and the diver, who was attached to us by the hoist cable. Willie was trying to drag the diver towards the lifeboat, which on its own was bloody dangerous, but we couldn't stay in position long enough for one of the crew to take the chance of jumping into the sea. Even though the lifeboat had a motor, it was simply not powerful enough to cope with the conditions. I was really worried about injuring the diver. If he got injured there was no way in hell we could rescue the crew. Just a small movement on the controls and in a split second I would be dragging him through extremely rough seas at twenty or thirty knots – faster than a water skier, and it would feel to me as if we were standing still.

I decided to lift the diver out of the water and move him, dangling fifty feet below us, back to the lifeboat, which had been blown a few hundred metres by now. I plonked him back into the water as close to the lifeboat as possible. Finally, one of the crew jumped into the water and within a few seconds, the diver had placed the strap around him and Willie was winding them up towards us. When the seaman scrambled on board, he had to be physically restrained he was just so happy.

That had taken ten minutes. I did another orbit while Willie and the diver shouted and waved their arms at each other, but it was not their fault. The conditions were way out of operational limits and a quick calculation revealed that we didn't have enough fuel to finish the job at this rate anyway.

I looked around for Jim but he had disappeared. Andy told me he had moved away to the east, to look for a tanker that had picked up the distress call from the Mauritius 2 and was travelling towards us. All this had come through on the radio while we were doing the rescue. In the chaos I had not even heard it, but Jiggs had responded while he was watching us battling our buns off with the hoisting.

Willie stuck his head into the cockpit and announced that we must give it another go. In all my time as a chopper pilot I had never seen a Navy diver back away from a task, so it worried me a bit that this could be fuelled by pride. Jim had found the tanker that was about thirty minutes away and a quick look at our fuel showed that we could wait for the tanker, and make it back as well. Ultimately it was my decision, so I said no. I was not going to take a diver back with concussion or broken bones for the sake of appearances.

Jim agreed, so we decided to loiter and wait for the tanker until our fuel state forced us to go home. I moved towards the stricken Mauritius 2 and did an orbit around it at two hundred feet. I had to admire the power of the sea as the swell crashed onto the deck, the spray cascading high into the air, every wave hammering a nail into the giant metal coffin.

Suddenly there was a noticeable change in the ship's attitude. The stern started sitting lower with foam visible inside the windows of the wheelhouse, and then the panes shattered spewing debris into the swell. The stern went down and the bow rose majestically upwards, almost vertical, so close to us that I could see the rusty links of the chains, fountains of spray hissing viciously out of the hull and the rolls of cable peeling off the deck and crashing into the sea. It stayed like that for what seemed ages, but it was probably just a few seconds, then it went down quickly, slipping backwards into the dark and leaving a massive pool of foam, oil and junk behind. I quietly cursed for not having my camera.

There was nothing to do now but wait for the tanker so we cruised around at 70 knots, the most economical speed in a Puma, orbiting the lifeboats in which the crew huddled together, no doubt wondering what was next.

When the tanker finally loomed out of the mist, they became quite animated and immediately the lifeboat turned and headed straight for it. I can only imagine how they felt. We watched as large nets were lowered onto the leeward side and one by one the crew clambered up the side to safety.

With the wind behind us we made excellent time back to Durban. I landed at Addington Hospital and dropped off our lone rescued seaman. Back at the base Major Foote told us he wanted us to stay and wait for the tanker to get into calmer water, and then hoist the remaining seamen off the deck. This meant we had to wait about three hours, but he would rather we finished the job off, so we sat around playing cards and chatting. Then I remembered that I was supposed to buy Van a ring, but that would have to wait for the next day.

After a few hours, the port authorities called us and advised that the tanker had requested the pick up immediately, because they had a nine kilometre turning circle and did not want to come any closer to Durban. So we set off again in better conditions and over a much calmer sea, to find the tanker not more than ten minutes out. Hoisting the crew was a piece of cake and within an hour we had dropped them off at Addington, so full of good cheer it was hard to believe they had just lost their ship.

❖❖

The following day the crew room was full for a change. We had visitors from Hoedspruit, a base where the Mirage pilots did their conversions and training, who were visiting Durban to practice low level air to air combat over the sea where their sonic booms didn't disturb anyone. They seemed to brief and debrief endlessly, strutting around in their "G" suits with hands full of notes and diagrams, all looking very serious. It always amused me the way they did a sort of weird, slow motion, kung-fu dance when they were discussing their aerial manoeuvres.

There were some thin lips on their part during the week, when a very irate Indian shop owner phoned in to the squadron complaining that an Air Force aircraft had flown so low over his shop that all the windows had broken. When asked what type of aircraft it was he said he was unsure, but it was the same shape as a *samoosa*. So from then on we called them *samoosa* pilots.

Peanuts came into the room and gathered all the chopper pilots up in one corner. “I need two commanders for a bush tour next month. They are going to attack a base near Ongiva and they need four extra Puma crews.” Ongiva was a town in Southern Angola that I had flown past many times.”I know we have spent a lot of time in the bush this year, but I guarantee the guys who do this tour will spend Christmas at home.” This seemed like a reasonable offer, considering I had spent eight months of the past year up there so far. Gone for a month and back for two weeks was the pattern, and I was feeling a bit stretched.

“Okay, I’ll go.” I volunteered.

“Yea me too.” Jim put his hand up. We gave each other a nod, and I was quite pleased we would be up there together.

We sat there chatting and Jim mentioned he had asked Sandy to marry him.

“So?” I looked at Jim expectantly.

“So what?” He was beaming. He knew what I wanted to know.

“Did she say ‘yes’ you prick?”

“Yep” he replied simply. I knew she would and I was genuinely chuffed for both of them. “And we want you to be best man.” Now that was great news and I accepted on the spot.

17

Ondangwa Ops

"A single arrow is easily broken, but not ten in a bundle"
Japanese proverb

I had still not bought the ring, but irrespective of that, twenty-four hours later we were unpacking our kit in Ondangwa. We had not even finished when a clerk came in and told us to hurry to the ops room for a casevac briefing. As it turned out, the operation would be delayed by a week so we would fit in with the daily tasks in the mean time, which was fine as it was very busy. No peace for the wicked as they say.

Jim and I did the casevac that was a routine pickup. A troopie had been bitten by a boomslang and he was in a shocking state – convulsing, delirious and his skin had turned a weird pinky-orange colour. The doctor had stabilized him by the time we returned, but I didn't give much for his chances. All we could do was hope for the best. Bullet wounds and broken limbs we knew, but snakebites were an unknown entity.

The next day we did trooping from an army camp close to the cutline called Ojiwarongo. Jim and I had a Puma each and we had to move a platoon about ten kilometres into Angola, where they would set up a temporary camp and do their patrols. We had a briefing with their ops officer and worked out that it would take six loads each to get the whole lot into position, including their rations and water.

We started up. I was ready first and took off immediately. It was only about five minutes flying time to the drop off zone and, if we got a move on, we could do the whole job without having to refuel. We took off and went straight there, landing between the trees of the area they had chosen to set up their camp. Jim settled in front of us and we watched as his load of troops jumped out. I noticed his engineer waving his arms at the troops getting them to hurry up and realized they wanted to take off ahead of us. There were two reasons for this: in this scenario the second chopper always had to land in the dust of the first one which made life a little uncomfortable, the other reason, more in character with my fellow pilot, was that Jiggs wanted a dice.

I told Duppie to chase the troops and he clicked immediately. As we lifted over the tree canopy I could see Jim was already pulling power and we set heading straight for the camp. If we had a rear view mirror he would have been tailgating us, but he could not overtake as he had to use the same cruise power setting as us, otherwise he would burn too much fuel for a marginal gain in speed. At the camp, the approach and flare to land was done with the utmost economy and Jim landed merely a few seconds after us. This went on for the remainder of the drops, with absolutely no advantage on either side as both of us were really *klapping it,* balancing speed and economy on a knife-edge that stretched our flying skills to the limit. The last pick-up was the food and water and I had been eyeing the two separate piles for the last few landings. The water that was packed in ten litre plastic bags was the smaller pile, but it was bulkier and more difficult to handle than the boxes of rations. Yet this was my choice, simply because there seemed less work in the handling. I landed right next to them and the loading began immediately with Duppie gesticulating and swearing at the troops to hurry. We lifted off while Jiggs still had a few boxes to load, so I had this one in the bag. When we landed in the bush camp, Duppie took the first bag and threw it onto the ground, but it burst, causing their officer to have a complete sense of humour failure. Suddenly the whole initiative went into slow motion as each bag was handled like a new-born baby. Jim landed and they simply dumped the boxes on the ground. I watched in dismay as he took power and lifted away, while we waited a few more minutes for the troops to finish. The victory was his.

The next day Jim and I and two gunships were called back to the bush camp before first light. They had been stonked during the night and a few of them had been killed and a number wounded. This was all too familiar as two years before my section had endured the same experience at Sifuma. I had watched deeply saddened as the bodies were loaded into the back wrapped in their ground sheets. Thoughts returned of Buis ordering us over the riverbank that night at the crocodile hole and we may have suffered the same fate but for his clear thinking.

Because the attack had happened at about four in the morning, there was a hunch that they may be waiting for the Pumas to arrive to attack again, hence the gunships. We spent the rest of the morning positioning stopper groups and later that afternoon contact was made. A two-day running battle ensued that involved the Alouettes and the troops, as they moved thirty kilometres to the north, finding a number of small weapons caches and stores of food as the enemy retreated. There was always a sense of wonder at SWAPO's crude methods, but they used their limited resources to enormous effect, using hit and run tactics over a large land area. They had the local population on their side, phenomenal bush skills and were very expensive to contain.

❖❖

The search and rescue procedures had been revised in order to reduce our time to the pick-up. The Impalas were very busy and getting shot at quite regularly and fortunately, during the few months leading up to the operation, none had been lost, but the law of averages and Murphy always played their hand when least expected. Because we were so much slower than the Impalas, roughly a third of the speed, we would follow them in a shorter circle and if one went down we would simply move from our circle to theirs – and their time on the ground would be reduced to about ten minutes, maximum fifteen, before they were rescued.

Jiggs and I were doing this procedure when one of the Impalas reported an engine failure and he was preparing to eject. He was about thirty kilometres inside Angola and we immediately turned over the cutline and headed towards him, waiting for an emergency beacon to start transmitting. Soon enough the needle on our indicator flickered and settled straight on the nose. Everything was going smoothly and it would be no more than ten minutes before the Impala pilot would be safely on his way home. We hardly needed the ELT because we could see the second Impala circling above his partner far in the distance.

When we got to the crash site, what we found was very interesting indeed. I landed and shut down as our stick of ParaBats melted into the bush to give us cover, while Jim flew up to the far edge of the *shonna.* I considered the spectacle of the "crashed" Impala. It was standing neatly with its flaps down and undercarriage extended without a scratch on it, and if it were not for the tube extending out of the cockpit and the hole in the canopy it appeared perfectly serviceable. Next to the aircraft was a man for whom I had been itching retribution, my long time antagonist Major Pine Pienaar. Now it was *my* turn to wind *his* neck in.

I slowly cast my gaze from the aircraft back along the *shonna* following the tracks the Impala had made in the sand over a distance of about a kilometre. No surveyor with the finest instruments could have scored three more perfectly straight and parallel lines on the sand. Next to the lines was a set of meandering footsteps that stopped next to the Impala. Far in the distance, I could make out the frame of the ejection seat and the parachute lying close to it. Pine had set the aircraft up to crash in the *shonna* and then ejected and the aircraft had done a flawless landing, pilotless it must be noted, and rolled to a stop all on its own.

"Lost any flying equipment major?" I asked innocently, alluding to the fact that he had lost his most valuable piece of equipment, his aircraft.

"Fuck you Lithgow!" he spat. I took a step back because I thought he was going to clobber me with his helmet. He looked as if an elephant had stood on him. "Now I suppose we'll have to burn this thing" he mumbled under his breath.

But I was not so sure. Standard procedure was to burn any stricken aircraft on the wrong side of the cutline to prevent them falling into enemy hands. There was probably only some minor technical fault that had caused the engine failure and all of its under wing stores, bombs, rockets and so on were missing, used by Pine on his mission, plus it would also be low on fuel. This meant it would be quite light and I wondered if we could lift it out with a Puma.

"What about the Frelon?" Jim piped up, and immediately there was light at the end of the tunnel. Pine cheered up noticeably, and Jiggs got on the radio to ask ops if there was any chance of collecting this one. There was a Super Frelon at Ondangwa that was on standby for the upcoming operation and they would be champing at the bit for some work. The Frelon was the largest chopper in the SAAF and could lift a lot more than the Puma, so we were sure they could recover this Impala. A few minutes later they replied that the recovery of the downed aircraft had been approved by ops at Oshakati and the Frelon, and two more Pumas carrying two extra sticks of ParaBats would be with us within the hour.

We found a spot in the bush and settled down to wait. Pine had come over all friendly and it was obvious he was hugely relieved that the Impala might be saved. He had been through a lot; ejecting would always be a very traumatic experience, and I had had my revenge so everything was equal to my mind.

It was almost an hour when we heard the distant beating of the choppers rotors. The ParaBats threw a smoke grenade and soon enough they thundered across the *shonna* and settled down next to us. The Frelon had a loading ramp at the rear that lowered and revealed a number of cables and hooks, that the ground crew lugged around and attached to the Imp at various mounting points. In less than twenty minutes, the Frelon started up and hovered so that the cables could be attached to the cargo swing. It gently lifted the Impala into the air, swinging around slowly in the downwash, and moved off towards Ondangwa. As the Frelon gathered speed, travelling slowly at sixty knots, the aerodynamics of the Impala pulled its nose into the direction of travel and the two of them and the four Pumas, with a platoon of ParaBats, acted as an escort. We had rescued a pilot, against which no value could be placed, and saved an aircraft worth many millions of Rands in less than four hours; a very impressive display of teamwork to be sure.

When I got back to our rooms later that night there was a penlight torch on my bed with a little note next to it. 'I thought this might come in handy,' said the note. It was signed by Pine. All was forgiven.

Our workload continued at a steady pace over the next few days. There were the routine trooping and re-supply tasks as well as few casevacs, and a very interesting trip to the Ruacana hydro-electric dam that had remained operational throughout the war, where we were shown the huge underground installation and the turbines spinning in a very business like fashion. SWAPO operatives had started blowing up the power lines and an Army base and airfield had been set up to protect the installation. While we were waiting for the two casevacs to be stabilized, the 110mm field guns in the camp fired a few salvos into Angloa – a very impressive display of raw power!

One night we took off and as we climbed out past the Ondangwa town a stream of tracers spat into the air, missing us by miles, but someone with an AK47 was having a go at us, or maybe just drunk and letting off some steam. This happened quite often, and the base was stonked every few months, always at night, and the perpetrators were never found. It was a bit unsettling to know that the enemy were so close to us and so difficult to pinpoint.

The next day we got instructions to collect a Puma crew from sixty kilometres inside Angola as their aircraft had been severely damaged. We found the Puma inside a terrorist camp that 32 Battalion had over-run, in the middle of a network of trenches with its tail boom broken off at the base. Other than that it was undamaged. Again the Super Frelon was summoned to bring a replacement boom and the aircraft was repaired right where it stood. My buddies looked a bit sheepish as this was the result of a hard landing with a full load, but it was also an indication of how hard the aircraft worked and that metal fatigue was a problem we might have to deal with.

A day later I had my own un-nerving experience. I was coming in to land in the bush with a stick of ParaBats when there was a huge bang. The Puma hit the ground and rolled for about sixty metres before it stopped. In the split second that followed I thought we had been hit by an RPG, but a locking pin from one of the air filters had come adrift and gone into the turbine where it had literally exploded. Luckily there were no trees in the way or we would have pranged for sure, so we flew the empty Puma back to Ondangwa on one engine, a nerve racking experience in itself.

Back at ops, I heard that the Mirages had arrived at Grootfontein and it was obvious that the operation was going to start within the next few days.

The next morning we took off for Eenhana to do a propaganda exercise involving the local population. At Eenhana we loaded two two-hundred litre drums into the back, a few cases of Russian military ordnance and a number of troops.

Our destination was only a few minutes flying away and we landed in an open area next to a traditional Ovambo village. The troops set the drums up at one end of the clearing and then opened the boxes to reveal two RPG launchers and a number of rockets. The locals were duly rounded up and one of the army officers explained, with the help of a translator, that the South African weapons were far superior, and indeed much more powerful than the SWAPO weapons. To demonstrate this we were going to fire rockets at the drums. Two launchers were produced, one looked brand-new and the other was badly chipped and scratched. Obviously the new one was ours, while the other, looking decidedly hammered, was the SWAPO weapon. I noted a few of the locals cooing and craning their necks at the goings-on. They had seen these weapons before, carried by SWAPO cadres during their incursions into Ovamboland, but probably never seen them fired.

An RPG was loaded into the SWAPO launcher and aimed at the drums at the other end of the clearing. What they didn't know, and neither did I, was that one drum was filled with water and the other with diesel. The troopie aimed carefully and fired. The rocket blasted across the opening with lightning speed, leaving a trail of white smoke and hit the one drum with phenomenal power, which burst into a great cloud of steam and tumbled backwards into the bush. The locals were impressed judging by the jabbering that was going on, and so was I, understanding immediately why this weapon was such a danger to choppers. Then the new launcher was loaded up and a big fuss was made of how superior and powerful it was. Again the troop aimed carefully and fired. What happened next was quite startling. The rocket flashed across the opening and hit the diesel drum right in the middle, which exploded with a massive roar and a great cloud of red flames and black smoke engulfed the trees behind it. Then one of the trees exploded into a ball of flames that mushroomed at least a hundred feet into the air. I was totally dumbstruck and the locals sprinted screaming into their village, many of them leaving their children behind.

When everything had settled down, the army officers called to the villagers to come back so that we could finish our exhibition, but they were having none of it. Eventually a message was sent through our interpreter that we could leave, preferably immediately, and no further demonstrations would be necessary.

The tree, as it turned out, was a Mopani that produced turpentine as a natural by-product. It was known to burst into flames during veld fires and whether the army guys placed the drum next to it on purpose or not remains a mystery. The propaganda exercise was judged to be a success and I had not had such fun in ages.

18
Omapanda

"He who rides the tiger shall fall and be eaten"
Kung Fu Tse

The next morning after breakfast we went straight into the briefing room. My heart sank when I looked at the map hanging in front of us. We were going to hit Omapanda.

They had obviously been planning Operation *Varknek* for quite some time. *Varknek* (pig's neck) was the nickname given to the local SWAPO commander in whose honour this exercise was to be conducted, bless his poor miserable soul. He was to enjoy the full contingent of Air Force services as well as the armoured corps, artillery, the ParaBats and 32 Battalion. We settled down for a full three hours as the plan unfolded and each detail was covered over and over again. With such a mixed bag of forces the margin for error was substantial, so co-ordination and communication was essential. Even with my limited experience of these operations I knew how quickly things got bent out of shape. The secret was to keep it simple.

Omapanda was a sort of transit camp for the gooks that was positioned just out of range of our artillery, quite close to Ongiva, the district capital in Southern Angola. It had an airfield that could handle a Hercules sized aircraft and a road feeding it from the north that was in good condition. It had always been a hot spot and over the years it had matured to the point of being a full-blown bush base. When we rescued Aubrey Bell, a few months earlier, we had been blasted with everything from AK47s and RPGs to 23mm anti-aircraft guns. There was a rumour that they also had 57mm recoilless cannons and even T54 tanks there. The plan seemed simple and comprehensive – our forward base was going to be Etale and the chopper fuel, ammo and Ratel armoured troop carriers were already in position.

When the briefing was over we all walked down to the pool for a chat and some coffee, but the guys were very subdued. It was clear to quite a few of us, particularly the more experienced pilots, that this was going to be a shitfight of some magnitude.

❖❖

The attack started at first light. The Ratels had moved up the road to the cutline at the Angolan border and then through the bush on their way to secure the southern flank of the camp. The ParaBats were going to be para-dropped on the eastern side next to the road from low level. Our job was to position stopper groups on the western boundary, on the web of footpaths and tracks that led to the camp, whereas the Alouettes would act as a stopper group on the northern side to prevent any movement to and from Ongiva.

The idea was to hit them hard from the air, then move the Ratels in, secure the camp and then get the ParaBats to sweep the camp, from the road in the east, to flush the enemy into the stopper groups to the west and north.

First light was at six, so we took off with the first load of 32 Battalion troops in the darkness before sunrise. We had to be extra careful not to fly too close to Omapanda and give the game away. Fortunately the Puma has a very low noise signature so we could get reasonably close to the camp without them hearing us, unlike the Alouette that has a very distinctive high pitched whine that can be heard from many kilometres away, but they would not be involved in the contact until later.

As we crossed the cutline into Angola, the horizon was beginning to light up and four Mirages passed overhead, disappearing into the darkness. The game was on.

Within a few minutes the first bomb flashes lit up the horizon, and there was a short break as the Mirages turned and did their second run in. The "Miracles" always made me shiver. They were so beautiful in the air and looked like black darts spitting fire as they swooped down on their targets with lightning speed. This time it was napalm, but the ack-ack ground fire had also started and the tracers were arcing into the air from the tree line, seemingly in a random fashion. They had obviously been taken by surprise and were panicking. Then the napalm struck and swept through the trees in colossal plumes of orange and yellow flames. A few seconds after this massive fireworks display, the ground fire stopped completely, like a stricken animal gasping for breath, as the enemy desperately sought a response. On the third run in they shot rockets and peppered the area with machine gun fire. The ground fire got quite intense as the enemy shot blindly into the air at aircraft they couldn't see. It was impossible to imagine the hell they were enduring on the receiving end of those Mirages.

With the help of the Forward Air Controller in a Bosbok high above us, we found our drop off point quite easily using the burning camp as a reference, just as the second pair of Impalas arrived and started their attack. As we took off to collect the next section of troops I almost felt sorry for the poor bastards in the camp. The whole area was smoke and flames and their shooting still seemed totally uncoordinated, although my spine tingled when the 23mm ack-ack tracers started streaming into the air. They were getting their act together and I wasn't looking forward to the return trip.

Spanner, the Bosbok pilot, started chatting to the two C130s as they droned past at about five hundred feet, guiding them onto the drop zone upon which a stream of ParaBats spilled out, like little mushrooms disappearing into the bush.

The trip back to Etale was about fifteen minutes and, with the light improving, I flew back down the road. Soon we were heading back to the camp with the next section of troops. By now there was a large amount of smoke billowing out of the bush. The Impalas had followed the Mirage onslaught and their attack was almost over as the Ratels started their thrust from the south. There was quite a lot of chatter on the radio from the Alouettes who had got into position in our absence and were soon blasting away at the gooks, as they fled into the bush to the north. Occasionally a large plume of fire and smoke erupted out of the trees as the fuel tank of a truck or a box of ammo was hit. Just as I was coming in to land there was a very large explosion in the camp that threw debris high into the air and our Puma bumped gently as the shockwave passed. An ammo dump got hit and anyone within fifty metres of it would have been blown to pieces.

Then I heard a chilling sound – the 'pok'-'pok' of bullets hitting the chopper as I flared, putting the Puma down as fast as I could. We hit the ground with a thump and the 32 Battalion troops were out in a flash, firing into the bush. I took off as an RPG flashed past our nose and exploded in the trees next to us. I banked hard left and headed away from the camp for a few seconds to get clear of the shooting. The radio was so busy I couldn't call Jim, but he would have landed a bit further away when he saw us drawing fire.

Then it was back to Etale for the last load of troops. As we skimmed over the trees I thought about how smoothly this op was going and the chances of getting it over with in one day. All the better for getting back to Durban and Van before the weekend.

When we landed we looked over the chopper for any serious damage caused by the bullets and discovered that the fuel bowser was missing. An ops clerk told Jim and I that we were wanted urgently in the ops room, so we went to see the boss while Willie and Jake started filling up with drums, which took at least an hour normally, so whatever had happened to the bowser had finally screwed up our plans. All the Pumas would need fuel and the Alouettes would be getting low as well, so the available drums wouldn't last very long at all.

The fuel bowser, amazingly, had followed the Ratels into the bush. As it turned out, the driver couldn't understand why he was the only vehicle left, so he tagged along, and no one had noticed in the darkness. Why anyone would knowingly drive a full fuel bowser into combat escapes me, but that was the first sign that things were going to get bent out of shape.

Another thing was that our landing zone had been changed. Floppy and Brian in the Alouettes had reported the enemy moving rapidly to the north-west using the network of tracks, so they were considering placing stopper groups on the main road to Ongiva and were working out the new positions for the drop-offs.

Then another more disturbing call came through. A Ratel had been hit and the crew had casualties. Jim and I would be refuelled first so it was our casevac and it sounded as if we would have to land right next to the camp.

Etale was beginning to look like a chopper parking lot and the MAOT had started diverting them to Eenhana, another camp a bit further south. It was packed with thirsty aircraft and there would be more arriving shortly. There was a strong possibility of running out of drums before the bowser got back.

After taking off we could see the smoke from Omapanda had spread over a wide area as the camp and the surrounding bush burned.

The scene in the camp was shocking. As I was coming in to land we flew over a large number of burnt-out trucks and equipment, some of it smashed and charred beyond recognition. The whole area was littered with bodies, some of them torn limb from limb. We landed next to the Ratel and one of the troops signalled us to shut down. The Ratel had apparently stalled and a 23mm ack-ack gun, hidden in the bush about thirty metres away, had simply lowered its sights and shot it full of holes. Of the fourteen guys on board only one had survived, miraculously unscathed, but he looked shocked out of his wits as he was guided like a zombie into our Puma by the medics. I dreaded looking into the Ratel but I had to do it. The troops didn't stand a chance. It looked like a human blender had blown up and smeared its contents all over the inside … …

What little was left of the troops was dumped into the body bags lying on the ground next to me. My feelings of nausea and rage were overwhelming.

We flew them back to Oshakati and refuelled at Ondangwa, a round trip of about two hours. When we got back to Etale, our last stopper group had long since been positioned, but we got a call to land at the northern end of the Omapanda camp and wait for instructions.

The initial attack by the Impalas, and the follow up by the Ratels, had been so devastating that it had not been necessary for the ParaBats to sweep the camp, so they sat around smoking and chatting at various spots next to the road with some of them waving cheerfully as we flew past. Had it not been for the Ratel, this would have been a very comprehensive victory because it seemed we had little more than light casualties among the other divisions. 32 Battalion had been very active for the first hour and had not suffered one single wounded, whereas the ParaBats had little more than a few twisted ankles and bruises after parachuting into the bush.

After landing we strolled around the camp looking at the mess. The tents, camo nets and all the equipment seemed old and well worn, almost like the leftovers from another war. Even the uniforms on the dead gooks were shabby and their AK47s dirty. Sunday would have had a heart attack within thirty seconds of seeing this place, but that said all their gear was fully functional and no less dangerous than any of our stuff.

It was very noticeable how young some of the terrorists were. They looked no more than fifteen years old, just kids, and most of them probably didn't even understand what they were doing there. SWAPO were well known for kidnapping young boys from the schools in Owamboland, then training and indoctrinating them to fight against us. For all we knew a local person working at Ondangwa could have their own child waging war against them.

Back at the Puma, Willie was loading long boxes on to the chopper that contained the rockets for the Stalin's Organ rocket launcher. They were all hidden in underground bunkers, invisible from above and might not even have been found had it not been for a Ratel collapsing one of the roofs. They were obviously planning a long range attack in the near future.

While we were standing around chatting, one of the other pilots mentioned that Spanner's Bosbok had taken a 23mm round through his elevator and he seemed to think it came from an area west of the main camp. Yet there was no intelligence indicating an enemy installation in this area so it seemed a bit odd.

We spent the rest of the day carting the rockets and other equipment back to Ondangwa and finished with a debriefing at sunset. The op had been a huge success and the body count was well over two hundred, not including the many still lying in the surrounding bush. In addition, massive amounts of equipment were captured or destroyed. An enquiry had been ordered into why the destroyed Ratel had stalled and there was a rumour that the gearbox had failed, but it was too late now.

The briefing the next morning was pretty much the usual stuff with one interesting difference. An aerial photo of the target area showed a tree line bordering one of the *shonnas* concealing a line of anti-aircraft guns. The emplacements seemed quite crude which meant that whatever they were protecting was new. Our job was to re-position the stopper groups, so Jim and I planned our route further to the west using a long thin *shonna* as a reference. We were in groups of two Pumas with a stick of ParaBats each and me flying lead.

The Alouette gunships, who were to provide top-cover for the operation, flew off in groups of two and because we were so much faster than them, we had to wait about half an hour for them to position before we took off. The butterflies were getting to me, as they always did before this sort of thing, even though the punch up was basically over.

At last ops told us to go. All eight Pumas started up together, and we set off in a big V formation until we got to the cutline where Jim and I peeled off to the northwest. We flew as low as possible over the tree tops and as we got close to the target area, I found myself flying even lower until I was worried about the aerials underneath the chopper hitting the tops of the trees. In the distance I could see our two gunships circling at a thousand feet.

"Jumbo 1 and 2 five minutes out," I called over the radio.

"I'll call you visual Nick," Danie replied. "There's nothing going on here," he added, referring to the target area.

The long *shonna* came into view and I had decided to stay over the trees, so I banked slightly left to keep away from the open space. Then I noticed something strange. The trees ahead seemed to be shimmering, and I jolted with fright when I realized it was groundfire. I banked hard right just flying through the edge of the muck and heard a few bullets hitting the chopper. I could see Jim behind me skirting the edge of the *shonna*.

"We're drawing fire!" I shouted over the radio, but Jim didn't have time to answer. A thin line of smoke shot out of the trees and hit his Puma at the root of the tail boom which separated and tumbled into the sand. For a moment it seemed to hesitate, then it pitched and rolled simultaneously, hit the ground inverted and erupted into a ball of flames and debris that would fill a stadium. I watched this with utter disbelief. My over-riding impulse was to turn round and pick Jim up. Shocked to the core, I realised my best buddy had been shot down.

We had our own crisis to deal with. Our main gearbox had taken a bullet and boiling hot oil was spewing all over the ParaBats in the back, who were shouting and cursing in the mess. It was a miracle no one fell out of the open doors.

"Jim's gone down!" I croaked over the radio.

"*Ja* Klaus … I know," Danie replied grimly, *"Ek gaan hulle nou moer!"* The gunships were heading towards the crash. The gooks now had to answer the call of two 20mm cannons.

The stench of smoke from the burning oil was making me choke and I glanced into the back to see what was going on. Willie, spattered with oil, was looking at a small triangular hole in the bottom of the main gearbox that was belching smoke. Now we only had a short time left in the air before our gearbox destroyed itself, so I decided to head back to Etale, the closest camp to the cutline. Accompanying the smell was the sound of grinding metal and I was watching the gauges and flashing warning lights like a hawk.

We made it with the gearbox on its last legs. After we shut down I walked around the Puma looking at the damage, still unable to grasp that Jim and his crew were dead. The oil sodden ParaBats sat around in silence. They had just lost fourteen of their buddies. It could so easily have been us.

❖❖

The next day was exhausting. My mind was churning with anger and grief, questioning why, why, why? What about Sandy and Jim's family and what about Van and my parents? They were all going to be devastated. To make it worse I was totally unmotivated and just wanted to sleep.

My crew were put onto casevac standby to give us a break, but I knew it would only be a matter of time before we would have to pick someone up from the contact area. There had been another big punch-up with the gooks after Jim got shot down, but as usual they just evaporated into the surrounding bush. We discovered the anti-aircraft positions indicated on the aerial photographs of Omapanda were nothing more than poles cut from the surrounding trees and painted black. They knew our aerial photos would pick up the decoy and that would make us to fly further west – over the real guns. It worked. I also realized that if the fuel bowser had not gone into the bush with the Ratels, we would have dropped our last stopper group right in front of the real ack-ack guns. But the ground troops had taken over the positions with relative ease and recovered a modest amount of weaponry. It was a small camp, and certainly didn't justify the loss of seventeen men and an irreplaceable chopper.

"Casevac crew to the ops room," a voice crackled over the intercom. I wasn't looking forward to this one. We took off and retraced the flight path of the previous day and I found myself flying perilously low over the trees.

"Watch out for the aerials," Willie commented. In recent history these HF radio antennae had become a regular cause for concern. After the cutline it got worse. I felt as if we were being watched, aimed at, extremely vulnerable. I had that un-nerving feeling that any second the shooting would start again, just as I did when we got stonked at the crocodile hole. My nerves were absolutely finished.

Soon the long *shonna* came into view. As we crossed over the tree line I saw the mangled and charred skeleton of the big cat lying in the sand, spread over a wide area. I banked low over the *shonna* and passed over a splintered rotor blade. It lay a few hundred metres away from the wreck indicating the fury of the impact.

We landed close to the army Buffels and shut down while the medics jumped out to look at the injured troopie. Jim had been shot down right next to a camp that we didn't even know was there. Aerial reconnaissance had missed it, or they had been misled by the poles next to the other *shonna*. Through the trees I could see equipment lying around with camo nets draped over some vehicles and a couple of small tents; it could only have been occupied by twenty or thirty troops. The only recognizable thing left of the Puma was the tail boom. I wondered what was left of Jim.

❖❖

The atmosphere in the pub that night was subdued. In one corner three beers stood untouched for Jim and his two crewmen, a tradition of ours showing respect for lost airmen. The whole base seemed to be under a cloud. Jiggs had become an integral part in my SAAF career and I could not imagine a day without his constant cheerfulness and his lunatic sense of humour. His co-pilot was the son of one of our senior officers, also a very popular guy, and his engineer was one of the longest serving airmen in the Air Force. I just couldn't get my mind around it.

"Do you remember me, lieutenant?" I looked around to find a very young troopie with a big smile on his face. "You picked me up the other day when I got bitten by a boomslang." This was indeed a surprise considering he was in such bad shape and I didn't think he would make it. "Please thank the other guys in the crew for me."

"Sure" I said, and left it at that.

❖❖

The next day I flew back to Waterkloof and was lucky enough to get a lift on our old SAAF Viscount back to Durban. The large number of fatalities had been in the papers so Van already knew about Jim's death. When I phoned her we had a sort of monosyllabic conversation and I knew immediately things were not going to be the same. That night when we got together she said she had had enough. The constant worry as well as never knowing when I was going away had bugged her from day one, but she had never said a thing, and now losing Jim was just too much. I was very upset, but I understood. I told her of my plans to do other things in the SAAF, but she wanted me to stop flying immediately, which was simply not possible. In two days I had lost my two best friends.

19
The Funeral

"Most of us die with much of our beautiful music still in us, un-sung, un-played"
Grant M. Bright

There were so many cars outside it took a while to find parking and Jim's service had already started when I entered the church. The church was packed, a sea of blue uniforms and I saw Sandy, sobbing uncontrollably, with Van sitting next to her looking so small and vulnerable. Their tears contrasted starkly with the last time I had seen them. And then Jim's family, absolutely devastated. His Dad looked up as I passed and gave me a nod. I never wanted my Dad to look like that. I had not seen Van again since we broke up a week before and I desperately wanted her to give me some sort of acknowledgement, but already she seemed like a stranger.

The service was just a blur. Normally a gathering of aircrew this big would incite great festivities but we just sat in silence, lost in our thoughts. At the end of the service a group of us went forward and picked Jim's coffin up and put it onto our shoulders. As we walked down the aisle I felt a gentle wave of energy pass over me that was so subtle it made my spine tingle and I knew somehow that Jim, although no longer with us, was fine.

Outside we placed Jim onto a field gun and draped the coffin with our Air Force flag. The gun and the *gharry* that was towing it were polished so brightly that they glinted in the sun and people stopped and stared as the procession passed, no doubt wondering who commanded such gravity.

At the cemetery Jim made the last part of his journey to his place of rest, carried shoulder-high by about a dozen of us, each of us needing to be part of the farewell. We lowered him into the ground, and in the background I heard the familiar whine of a Puma's turbines accelerating with the beat of the rotors. We stood in silence as the Puma took off, circled and then flew very low over the ceremony, the ground shaking as it thundered past. I stepped forward and picked up a flower that had fallen out of a wreath, silently I dropped it onto the top of my best buddy's coffin.

20
General Flying Sortie

"Don't pick your nose on finals"
SAAF joke

I left the Air Force three months later and was posted to 17 Squadron at Swartkops to serve out the balance of my contract as a Citizen Force pilot flying Alouettes. This was great, because I could get my teeth into my new job in Johannesburg and still maintain contact with my mates in the SAAF, as well as fly choppers and get paid for it. To remain current on the Alouette I had to fly nine hours every three months, so I planned to fly every Friday afternoon when things were quiet at work.

It was one such Friday afternoon when I was sitting in the crew room with a cup of coffee getting ready for a general flying (GF) sortie. Dave, one of my instructors, asked me if I could drop him off at Lanseria, another airfield about thirty kilometres to the west. He had lost a portable radio while doing an op at Ondangwa and he thought one of the guys at Lanseria may have picked it up. This was sort of en route to the general flying area, so I was happy to help him out.After attending to all the formalities we took off and headed out low level towards Lanseria. Flying the Alouette was always a joy. It has to be physically flown all the time without the aid of gyro stabilisers and auto-pilot, aided only by a simple hydraulic actuating system. If you let go of the controls, it literally fell out of the sky and because the Alouette is so responsive, your control inputs consist of hundreds of tiny hand movements that become instinctive after a while. You don't actually fly it, but feel it and understand it, to the point where the Alouette becomes an extension of your mind and body. Also, it has one of the best power-to-weight ratios of any chopper ever built – not bad for an aircraft that is almost fifty years old. However, as I mentioned earlier, it is quite slow and tends to fly slightly right wing low, using a piece of string dangling in the wind to help the pilot keep the chopper straight in the air. It's as tough as nails though and as an airborne workhorse, it's second to none.

Lanseria was about a ten minute flight and as the airfield came into view, I called the control tower. We flew straight in to the 44 Squadron dispersal area and I decided not to shut down, so Dave hopped out and ducked under the clattering rotor blades. I had to pick him up on the way back from the GF, so there was about an hour for him to find his radio, and for me to hone my flying skills.

We took off again and I set the radio frequency on 119.7 for the general flying area. Heading north, I climbed gradually in the smooth air as the majestic Magaliesburg range rose up before us. As we reached the crest, we were sharing the sky with such distinguished company as eagles and vultures soaring effortlessly on the thermals.

On the other side of the range the land flattened onto a rocky plateau, which is where we practiced our mountain flying. There were also a few drums up there filled with concrete of different weights that we used for cargo swinging and hoisting practice. We went through the drills and practiced a few slope landings, all of which demanded a high level of teamwork with my flight engineer and some very accurate flying and concentration on my part. The air was quite a lot thinner up there which affected the performance of the Alouette, so everything needed a bit more time and space. There are a lot of streams that cascade over the rocks into small gorges and dam up into pools of water. It's all very picturesque and it's a very popular area for hikers and nature lovers.

Next we decided to fly around Hartebeespoort Dam, which was in the valley a thousand feet below, and then I did one of my favourite tricks. I flew very low along the plateau, towards the escarpment and, as we got to the edge, I pushed the nose down, so for a few seconds we were weightless as the Alouette did a controlled plunge into the valley. Most of the battle hardened engineers never flinched, but the new guys or anyone that came along for a flip generally shrieked with terror or delight, I'm not sure which. I just loved the feeling.

The dam was full for a change and clear of water lilies so we flew around admiring the scenery for a while, and I practiced a few short-stop landings along with some hovering on one of the grassy beaches. Then it was time to head back, so I took off and made for a gap in the hills that led directly to Lanseria. Once in the gap, I realised we were in a small flat valley that rose gradually in front of us and, as I tried to keep the speed up, I found myself flying quite close to the ground. I knew the airfield was getting close, so I took my hand off the collective for a second and flicked the radio frequency over, while watching like a hawk for windmills and telephone lines that are always a danger when flying so low. As we exited through the gap I could see the airfield in the distance and called the tower. As far as I can remember the conversation went something like this.

"Tower, this is hotel-four-one-alpha returning from the GF low level, airfield in sight, request joining and landing instructions."

"Hotel-four-one-alpha, we do not have you in sight, call runway three-five visual next," was the reply. I did not know Lanseria very well so I was hacking it and figured that, being in a chopper, I could get away with it. I could see the runway and the control tower looming in front of me and I was a little surprised they could not see me.

"Runway visual," I called back flatly as I was getting close now and did not want to go bombing in without them knowing where I was.

"Hotel-four-one-alpha you are still not visual, what is your position?" I was now only a few hundred metres away, and decided to err on the side of caution so I replied, "Hotel-four-one-alpha orbiting to port, can you see me now?" I banked the Alouette left into a slow turn, playing for time.

"Negative." This was not possible but I carried on with the turn, climbing a bit to help the controller and, as I levelled off, I called again.

"Can you see me now?"

"Negative." This was ridiculous and by now I had the distinct impression they were buggering me around, so I decided to call their bluff and headed straight for the tower. I flared dramatically and went into the hover a few metres from the sloping glass windows, and stared at three guys looking back at me. Below me the chopper downwash was causing a dust storm at the entrance to the departure hall, and a well-dressed lady was having her clothes trashed and her luggage blown away. I deliberately prolonged the time before my next call to heighten the effect.

"Can you see me now?" I asked with pointed indignation, staring the three guys in the tower straight in the eye.

"Negative, please check your frequency." My heart sank as I realised that something was very wrong. I glanced down at the radio and realised I was speaking to Waterkloof about thirty kilometres away. Negligence on my part, and fate, over which no man has any control, had combined to strike a cruel blow and my reputation was ruined in one brief radio call. I was on 124.7 and I was supposed to be on 124.0. The mistake began with the GF frequency and my low flying had caused me to miss it. I reached down and changed the frequency.

"Lanseria tower, hotel-four-one-alpha, good day," I spluttered, wishing I could crawl under my seat.

"Aaaah-ha, hotel-four-one-alpha, a very good morning to you sir! Please proceed to SAAF dispersal at your leisure," was the silky reply. My engineer and the two other guys in the tower, who I could see clearly through the glass, were having a fit.

I was flushed with embarrassment and furious with myself, and I really wished I didn't exist. I air taxied the short distance to the dispersal area and landed near Dave, who had been viewing this from a distance with a very puzzled look on his face. We took off again after some very polite radio procedures and made for Swartkops. By the time we landed I was famous. The guys at Lanseria tower had obviously reported this outrageous breach of procedures. I thought I was going to walk the plank, but our ops officer was highly amused, as was the rest of the squadron and the penalty was no more than a bottle of Scotch. What was written in my personal file I will never know, but it was sure to be interesting reading. I suspect the files of a lot of chopper pilots tended to be more entertaining than the norm.

These legends tend to follow you around for a long time in aviation, sometimes a lifetime, so I was anxious to keep it quiet. But there is always a lesson to be learned from these little disasters. I have a phobia about radio procedures now and understand why air traffic controllers get so ratty with pilots at times.

21
Casevac et al

Beware the enemy within

Things went quite smoothly during my first year in civvy street. I enjoyed my new job, although it didn't involve any flying, and managed to buy a small house and settled down to a relationship with my new girlfriend, Karen. I still had regular contact with my friends in the military, as once a year I had to do a bush tour for a few weeks. So yet again, I found myself packing for the border.

Top cover at Ondangwa was generally a boring job that entailed flying an Alouette gunship around the base at about a thousand feet, while the Flossie, either a Hercules C130 or a Transall C160, did a spiral descent from high altitude. They had been shot at in the past by small arms and RPGs, but the real danger was from the Sam 7 shoulder launched anti-aircraft missile that, although obsolete and limited in its ability, could bring down a Hercules if it got hit in the right place. The idea of top cover was to keep the enemy's heads down while all this was going on, and it would have been a very foolish gook who fired anything more than a peashooter with a gunship around.

We took off as the sun was rising through the storm clouds on the horizon, giving me a stunning colour display of blues, greys and pinks with shafts of silver beaming through the gaps. I climbed a bit higher to enjoy the view and watched the ever impressive C130 droning gracefully past, banking steeply to maintain the spiral and lowering the flaps and landing gear as it prepared to land. Once it was on the ground I descended and landed back on the dispersal area.

I shut down and was busy gathering my gear, when a Military Policeman (MP) walked up to me and introduced himself. This was unusual because we seldom had anything to do with them as they kept very much to themselves. His uniform was spotless with creases like razor edges. He looked very well groomed and certainly not as if he was roughing it on border duty. I found them to be generally aloof, even arrogant at times because they tended to neglect saluting and rank, almost as if these things were beneath them. This bloke was no different. He told me briefly that there was a casevac at one of the bush camps and a troop was in some sort of trouble. He had been sent to investigate the incident and I was to provide the necessary transport.

To save a bit of time, I switched on the gunship's radio and called the ops room. The officer on duty answered and said I should leave immediately as the casevac was serious.

I quickly went to sign the authorization book while my engineer Andre got the utility Alouette ready. Soon we set off for Etale, a camp quite close to the cutline that was always a hot spot for terrorist activity.

We flew low over the trees for about twenty five minutes. By this stage I navigated more by instinct, picking up the occasional landmark and seldom needing a map. Eventually Etale came into view, a patch of white sand next to the main road coming down from Angola and, to my surprise, the MP asked me to land outside the camp as he might have to do an investigation and he did not want sand blown all over the evidence. So I picked a spot near the camp entrance and put the Alouette down gently, as a big cloud of dust swirled up around us. I shut down and he disappeared into the camp, accompanied by a few of the camp's officers muttering among themselves in subdued tones.

Andre and I waited patiently at the chopper for at least a half hour. It was obvious that there was quite a bit of drama and whatever had happened was being handled very carefully.

At last a medic appeared and greeted us respectfully. He looked inside the Alouette for a while scratching his head and then went back into the camp. Next came four troops labouring with a body bag. My heart sank. This sortie was beginning to take a form I did not like. They looked at Andre questioningly and the only way we could get the body in was to lay him cross-wise on the rear floor, which they did under Andre's supervision. There was also a small bag with his personal effects that was placed on the edge of the doorway and during the struggle to place his body, one of the troops bumped it accidentally and it fell to the ground. Its contents emptied onto the sand.

Suddenly it was no longer a body in a bag, but it was a real person who had lost his life. There was a photo of his girlfriend, his razor and well-worn wallet, a copper bracelet, a small pen knife and a carved wooden figurine that was probably a good luck charm. We all stood for a few seconds staring at this lot, none of us wanting to pick it up, too moved and not willing to handle a dead man's personal things. Finally I bent down and placed the bits and pieces back in the bag, more to cover my overwhelming sadness than anything else.

We stood next to the Alouette in an awkward silence for what seemed ages and then at last the MP appeared, guiding a tall thin troopie by the arm, followed by the officers all looking very gloomy. I doubt if he was a day over eighteen and he looked much younger in his forlorn state. His face was the colour of ash, his head and shoulders drooped as he stared blankly at the ground and his eyes were red from crying. The MP was talking to him in a hushed tone and he followed the instructions meekly.

Without being told I knew what had happened. This bloke had shot his buddy by accident. An accidental discharge was one of the most devastating ways to lose a soldier and one where the enemy didn't even have to pull the trigger.

The MP indicated for the troopie to take his place on the rear seat, which in a military Alouette was a plank of plywood fitted into a metal frame. He did so and was then at a loss as to where to place his feet. The MP told him to put them on the body, which he did and then started sobbing uncontrollably. He hands were then handcuffed to the seat frame and he sat there perched with his hands between his legs and his skinny knees next to his shoulders, tears streaming down his face.

We climbed in and I started up. I looked in the back before take-off and noticed the MP had placed himself to the right of the troopie and had loosened the holster of his sidearm. This seemed a bit extreme but I guessed he knew what he was doing. He had his procedures just as I had mine.

We took off and headed for home. The trip was very peaceful for the first ten minutes when the troopie started sobbing again, and it was clear he was in a very unstable state emotionally. He made so much noise I could hear him above the racket the chopper was making and I was wearing a helmet. I glanced around and the MP was sitting there with an indifferent look on his face, ignoring the troopie. It's possible he simply did not know what to do and, anyway, there is very little place for consolation in a military situation, however desperate.

We flew on for a while and then without warning the MP started shouting at the troopie, telling him to shut up, threatening to clobber him and throwing in a few insults about his mother to drive the point home. Under normal circumstances this would have been the usual disciplinary bluster but it made the troopie worse and he flopped down sideways on the bench seat with his head resting on the opposite door. This really upset the MP who shouted at him to sit up, and the next thing the troopie lashed out with his right foot and hit the MP square in the face, banging his head hard on the bulkhead in the process. Fortunately for the MP, they were sitting too close together for the troopie to have much leverage, but his nose started bleeding profusely and he looked dazed. Then the troopie kicked again, this time hitting the back of my seat. The MP grabbed his leg, and he swung the other one connecting the MP in the guts. The situation was out of hand. He brought his foot back for another kick and disaster loomed. His foot jammed between the middle seat and mine and I felt the collective lever jerk in my left hand as the Alouette dropped like a stone. Under normal circumstances this would not have been too serious, but we were flying just above the treetops. The ground came up so fast that my response was purely instinctive. I pulled the nose up and tugged desperately on the collective when suddenly it came free and we started lifting. I flew around a large tree at such an angle I thought the main rotor would hit the ground and realised that we had luckily descended into an open *shonna*. The troopie's foot was now free but he was still frenzied and the MP was starting to panic.

I'd had enough. I flared and dumped the power and we went into a controlled emergency landing. Within a few seconds we touched down and I turned around to shit on both of them, but the MP had slid the door open and leapt outside with his pistol drawn and pointed at the troopie. They were still screaming at each other with one drenched in tears and the other in blood. I told Andre to hold the cyclic as the chopper was still running at full power and got out as well. The MP was a very scary sight. His eyes were slits, his face puffed and smeared with blood and his hands shaking uncontrollably. Worse, his finger was on the trigger and the troopie was unrelenting, swearing and spitting at him. He was still locked to the seat so thankfully one of them could not move. For one terrible moment, I had visions of taking two bodies back to Ondangwa.

I put my hands out in front of me, palms facing him, and walked slowly forward, my mind racing with the consequences of this fiasco. It was an incredibly tense moment. He took a step towards the troopie and took aim. I noticed the slightest change in his eyes and I knew he was going to shoot. I jumped forward, slapping the gun down with all my weight and a shot went off. He fell back and we tumbled into the sand, both of us grappling desperately for the pistol as he punched me hard on the side of the helmet, which had no effect as it was designed for much worse trauma. I grabbed the pistol by the barrel and I was not letting go. I gave it a yank, knowing I would not get shot if it went off and he could not reload if it did, and as it came away the MP let off a howl of pain. There was blood pouring from a wound on his hand. When the shot went off the pistol's slide had caught the web of skin between his thumb and forefinger and I had torn it open.

What a mess this had turned out to be. I now had the gun, which was jammed, and the MP was standing in front of me shaking with rage. It seemed I had become his target. He took another swipe at me and stopped suddenly as I jumped up and moved quickly back to my seat, threw the pistol into the front of the Alouette at Andre's feet and picked up my R4 rifle. This sobered things up immediately. The MP lifted himself slowly off the ground and stood there looking at me like a kid that had been licked in a schoolyard scrap. I shouted for Andre to shut down.

After the rotors had stopped I gave them both hell. We had nearly crashed and besides nearly getting killed there was the matter of almost destroying an irreplaceable Air Force chopper. To cap it all, both were showing disrespect for a fallen comrade. This time I was taking no chances. Andre, who was swearing at both of them in a very military fashion, handcuffed the troopie to the one side of the cabin and attached the MP to the other using a cable-tie. They both accepted this in silence and before long we were airborne again, heading for Ondangwa.

After we had landed and shut down, the MP begged me not to take the matter any further. I looked at Andre to check his response and he did not seem too bothered. As I was not a stickler for discipline I made a deal. The MP was to report favourably on the troopie's behaviour and the troopie was to put his best foot forward in a bad situation. They both agreed and Andre and I let the matter rest.

They loaded the body bag into the back of a *gharry* and before they set off for Oshakati, I gave the MP his sidearm back and had to smile at the piece of skin dangling from the slide. What a sorry sight that MP was, covered in blood and dirt, his face full of welts and looking as if he had been in a bar brawl rather than a routine job. It was impossible not to gloat as I had never seen an MP with so much as a hair out of place.

A week or so later I was in the Ondangwa pub when someone tapped me on the shoulder. I turned around to find the MP, sparkling clean and tidy with a big smile on his face. He thanked me for not taking the incident further and advised that the troopie had been charged with involuntary manslaughter and was receiving counselling. The poor bloke who had been shot was a swimming champion and his buddy who shot him was a rowing partner from school. They only had two days to go before they went home. What a waste.

I don't have access to statistics but I reckon at least eighty percent of the casevacs we did had nothing to do with the enemy. Many involved guys that had shot themselves or their buddy accidentally and then there were road accidents, snake bites, burns and of course injury from enemy action and so on. But most of the injuries were accidental and could have been avoided.

22

Father Christmas

"The (Alouette) thundered in the South,
And with the sound
The carols drowned
Of peace on earth, good-will to men!"
Henry Wadsworth Longfellow

Unfortunately the pressure of my job in Johannesburg started affecting my responsibilities at the squadron and after a while it became difficult to remain current on the Alouette. I had a meeting with Crow, our Officer Commanding, and very reluctantly asked him to find me a posting that was easier to handle time wise. He made a few enquiries and advised that I was to be transferred to 92 Tactical Airfield Unit in the New Year, but that I still needed to continue my duties at the squadron until then.

So the last bush tour I did in the SAAF was at Rundu just before Christmas. Rundu was a very quiet base in those days situated roughly in the centre of the Caprivi Strip and we didn't have much to do flying wise, so the days were spent reading and playing cards, with the evenings spent in the pub. I jumped at any excuse to fly, so when I was asked to deliver Father Christmas to the camps kiddie's party in my Alouette, I was only too happy to oblige.

In typical military fashion everything was planned down to the last detail. I would take off with Father Christmas and then the kids and their moms would be taken on a large flat-bed trailer to the edge of the hardstand. I would then return, land in front of the trailer and drop him off with a big bag of presents and then take off again to get out of the way, because the noise of the chopper would unhinge the proceedings.

I did the pre-flight checks and Father Christmas duly arrived dressed in a very cheap, thin plastic suit, dripping with sweat in the heat. He climbed in the back with his bag of presents and it was then that I recognised Father Christmas as a very surly army major, a rather round man with swarthy skin and a thick black moustache. I didn't know him very well, but we exchanged pleasantries and I started up and took off, flying away from the base for a minute or so but close enough for me to see the trailer arrive at the hardstand in the distance.

After a few minutes it crept onto the hardstand and, even from a few miles away, I could see it was packed with people. I decided to do a bit of a dramatic approach, quickly in, dump him off and then take off as soon as he was out.

Everything went smoothly. I flared and put the Alouette down neatly, the door slipped open and he lumbered onto the hardstand with his bag of presents and the kids and moms cheering and waving their arms in delight. As soon as he was clear of the main rotor I took power and put the nose down, but Father Christmas had a problem. The rotor wash from my fancy take off pulled at his flimsy suit and suddenly it shredded, blowing away like confetti and leaving him standing there in front of his fans in his underpants and army boots! The only thing left of the suit was his snow white beard, contrasting starkly with his hairy body.

The kids recognised him immediately, all laughing and pointing at their *oom,* and there were a few red faces among the moms, but he took it in fine spirit. We became good buddies after that and shared many hours in the pub together.

Sadly, that was my last bush tour and the end of a fantastic phase in my flying career and it was such an overwhelming experience that I think about it constantly as I get older. I have flown many hours since then in a wide variety of civilian aircraft, but it's just not the same. Every hour flown, every operation, every task was completely different to the last and that variety is impossible to match in any occupation so I was spoilt beyond redemption in terms of flying. If I had my life over, in a heartbeat I would ask the Good Lord to make me a chopper pilot … again!